LIFE OF THE TRAIL 7 HISTORIC HIKES AROUND
MOUNT ROBSON AND THE SNAKE INDIAN RIVER

LIFE OF THE TRAIL 7 HISTORIC HIKES AROUND
MOUNT ROBSON AND THE SNAKE INDIAN RIVER

Emerson Sanford & Janice Sanford Beck

Canmore

Alpine Vista Publishers
145 Carey
Canmore, AB, T1W 2R3
403 609 3164
E-mail: emsanf@telus.net

Distributed by Alpine Book Peddlers
140 – 105 Bow Meadows Cresent,
Canmore, Alberta T1W 2W8
Phone: 403 678 2208, 866 478 2280
www.alpinebookpeddlers.ca
info@alpinebookpeddlers.ca

Library and Archives Canada Cataloguing in Publication

Sanford, Emerson
	Historic hikes around Mount Robson & the Snake Indian River /
Emerson Sanford & Janice Sanford Beck.

(Life of the trail ; 7)
Includes bibliographical references and index.
ISBN 978-0-9879270-0-2

	1. Hiking--British Columbia--Mount Robson Provincial Park--Guidebooks. 2. Trails--British Columbia--Mount Robson Provincial Park--Guidebooks. 3. Hiking--British Columbia--Mount Robson Provincial Park--History. 4. Robson, Mount (B.C.)--Guidebooks. 5. Hiking--Alberta--Jasper National Park--Guidebooks. 6. Trails--Alberta--Jasper National Park--Guidebooks. 7. Hiking--Alberta--Jasper National Park--History. 8. Jasper National Park (Alta.) -- Guidebooks. I. Beck, Janice Sanford, 1975- II. Title. III. Title: Mount Robson & the Snake Indian River. IV. Series: Life of the trail ; 7

GV199.44.C22B74825 2012	796.5109711'82	C2012-900545-2

Front cover photo: Mount Robson and Berg Lake. Photo © by Fred Vermeulen.
Back cover photo: Sketch by Dr. Cheadle showing the Milton and Cheadle party crossing a river.

Printed in Canada

Financial assistance from the Alberta Lottery Fund and the Alberta Historical Resources Foundation for the publication of this volume is gratefully acknowledged.

This book was produced using FSC-certified, acid-free paper, processed chlorine free and printed with vegetable-based inks.

DISCLAIMER

Hiking in the Canadian Rockies is a potentially dangerous activity. The trail guides in this book describe how to get from one place to another but do not deal with the issue of safe travel.

A hiker's personal safety depends on exercising good judgment and having the necessary skills, education and experience. In addition to outfitting oneself with the proper food, clothing and equipment, one must also be able to deal with unsafe trail conditions resulting from storms or other natural occurrences, the challenge of fording deep and fast flowing rivers and streams, injuries, the dangers of getting lost, encounters with wild animals and any other unexpected occurrences.

The authors and publishers of this book accept no responsibility for the actions of others. If you have any doubt about your ability to safely hike any route described in this guidebook, do not attempt it.

As we left Robson Station for Mt. Robson on the tenth of October all the Red Gods smiled upon us. No other time of the year could have been more alluring than this day in late fall in the Canadian Rockies when our little outfit of thirteen horses hit the trail leading among the yellow poplars on the flats and the flaming arctic bear-berries on the lower mountain-sides. No longer were they mountains of green forest, grey rock and white snow. They were literally ablaze with colour, from the frost-touched lower reaches of vegetation across the variegated rocky cliffs up to the sun-kissed, rosy peaks.

-Mary Jobe Akeley[1]

Contents

ACKNOWLEDGEMENTS

The preparation for a book of this type requires the perusal of many secondary sources; during our research we read hundreds of books. The authors of the books used are acknowledged in the Notes section at the end of this book. Many of the books are still in print and readily available. Others required much diligence on the part of reference librarians to obtain interlibrary loans, and we wish to thank the personnel at the Canmore Public Library, especially Michelle Preston and Hélène Lafontaine, for their assistance. Other books and documents were available only through the Whyte Museum and Archives and we appreciate the efforts of Lena Goon, Elizabeth Kundert-Cameron, D.L. Cameron, and Ted Hart for steering us on the right track and obtaining materials for us.

The authors appreciate the time that Graeme Pole spent providing very thoughtful comments regarding publication of the volume and the assistance of Edward Lovering, Fred Vermeulen, Cheryl Sanford, Shawn Sanford Beck, Chyla Cardinal and Andrea Petzold with images, maps, design, logo and proofreading. Monica at the Alpine Club of Canada in Canmore kindly allowed us the use of their collection of the Canadian

Alpine Journal and Meghan Power of Jasper Yellowhead Museum and Archives made a special effort to provide information on Major Fred Brewster. Others who provided useful discussion and/or materials during the course of the research were: Fiona Bradley, Royal Botanic Gardens, Kew, England; Debra Moore, Hudson's Bay Company Archives, Archives of Manitoba, Winnipeg; Sherry Bell, Reference Archivist, CMS Archives (City of Edmonton); and Betty Anne Muckle, grand-daughter of Andrew Sibbald who provided both images of her grandparents and information about their lives.

A large part of the effort in preparing the volumes in the Life of the Trail series was in hiking all of the trails and routes described in the history section. Emerson wishes to thank his wife, Cheryl, for the many hours she spent taking him to trailheads and picking him up several days later at a different location, sometimes on remote gravel roads that were not easily accessible. Cheryl always had in hand a copy of the itinerary for the hike in order to contact the Warden Service if the solo hiker did not emerge from the wilderness at the appointed time (he always did).

In addition, Emerson wishes to acknowledge the many hikers on remote backcountry trails who stopped to chat and made the solitary hikes more enjoyable. Many of these are mentioned in the text. There were also several wardens along the way who contributed to the enjoyment of the backcountry experience.

For Janice, this project has been a labour of love, squeezed in amongst various family, community, and work responsibilities. She would like to thank her partner, Shawn, and children, Rowan, Robin and Christopher, for their willingness to accommodate the time required for a project of this magnitude. She would also like to thank her parents for sharing their love of history and introducing her to the trails these volumes bring to life.

Financial assistance from the Alberta Lottery Fund and the Alberta Historical Resources Foundation for the publication of this volume is gratefully acknowledged.

INTRODUCTION

From season to season, year to year, century to century, the appeal of the Canadian Rockies remains undiminished. And while first-time visitors are perhaps most impressed, the majesty of the peaks is by no means lost on either return visitors or permanent residents.

What has changed over the course of time are the reasons people have come to the mountains and the length of time they have remained in their midst. Aboriginal peoples' travel through the Rockies was primarily inspired by the wealth of resources in the land between – and beyond – these lofty peaks. In the period before European contact, hunting and gathering excursions into the Rockies were common amongst peoples in the surrounding regions. And with peoples from the east and west both venturing into the region, it is not surprising that passes through the range became links in a vast network of cross-continental trade.

The second period of exploration in the Rockies – that of the fur-traders – was likewise motivated by the wealth of resources: in this case the fur-bearing animals that inhabited the region and the lands farther west. Traders like David Thompson, some of whose exploits are recounted in this volume, were keen to access the furs of the interior of today's British Columbia . With the assistance of Aboriginal guides, these traders sought out the most direct route of passage, seldom tarrying to explore.

The importance of the Yellowhead Pass as a fur-trade route did, however, mean that some officials set up residence at posts in the region. It also meant that the second and third periods of exploration overlap more extensively in this region than in most parts of the Rockies. The third period of exploration, that of the government scientists and surveyors, is generally held to have begun with the 1858 Palliser Expedition and lasted until the completion of the Canadian Pacific Railway in 1885. These industrious men were anxious to discover the region's mineral and agricultural potential, then to determine the most practical route for a cross-continental rail line, cutting trails as they went. In this region, the third period continued into the early twentieth century, as the more northerly Grand Trunk Pacific and Canadian Northern Railway lines were surveyed and developed, then merged into the Canadian National Railway in 1916, shortly after their completion.

Because of the area's distance from the CPR line, the fourth period of exploration, that of the tourist–explorers and mountaineers, began later in this region than in those farther south. It was only the most adventurous of these pleasure travellers who ventured into today's Jasper National Park before the completion of the Grand Trunk Pacific. Those who did were rewarded for their efforts with the opportunity to visit areas few non-Aboriginal people had seen before. This was the era of the pack train, when well-to-do travellers engaged outfitters to provide guides, horses, provisions and all the other equipment and assistance required to pursue their adventurous dreams.

Businesses sprang up to cater to their wishes and parks were established to protect the lands these early railway patrons wished to explore. Again, these developments had begun to the south, with the establishment of the Banff Hot Springs Reserve in 1885 and its 1887 expansion into Rocky Mountains Park. The Jasper Forest Reserve was established in 1907. Lewis

Swift was appointed the first game guardian of Jasper Park in 1910. A second warden, Alex McDougal, was hired in 1912. He became chief warden in 1914 with seven wardens serving under him. By 1915 there were nine wardens in Jasper.

In order to accomplish their mandate, these wardens needed trails from which to patrol the park. In 1913 over 40 miles (64 km) of trails were constructed or repaired in Jasper Park, with trail building concentrated near the townsite. During 1920–21, wardens supervised the construction of a 53-mile (85 km) trail from the Sunwapta River to the junction of the Southesk and Brazeau rivers. By 1939 the park boasted 624 miles (1004 km) of trails.

By that time, automobile use and lightweight camping gear had all but eliminated the need for the outfitters of the fourth period. Equipped with backpacks, lightweight tents and dehydrated food, hikers were able to follow established trails through the Rockies for long distances without need of horse or guide. Very few trails have since been established, the main exceptions being realignment or replacement of trails for environmental reasons and small extensions built to divert hikers from river crossings suited only to horses. Because the adventures of these modern travellers are far too numerous for us to recount, our narrative comes to a close at the dawning of this era.

The *Life of the Trail* series divides historic routes throughout the Rockies into regions based primarily on geographical boundaries that influenced nineteenth-century travellers. The series presents volumes in order of entry by non-Aboriginal explorers, and routes within each volume are described in order of first use. Each book, designed to fit neatly into a pack, outlines the history of the routes in its region, giving modern day travellers a feel for how they were established and who has used the trails since.

Life of the Trail 1 records historic routes and hikes in the area bounded by the North Saskatchewan River on the north and the Mistaya River, Bow River and Lake Minnewanka on the west and south. The most historically significant trip in this area was David Thompson's journey along the Red Deer River to meet the Kootenay people and take them back to Rocky Mountain House. Later, the Aboriginal route over Pipestone Pass to the Kootenay Plains was used extensively by tourist-explorers and mountaineers. Today this area is bounded by the David Thompson Highway (#11) in the north and the Icefields Parkway (#93), the Bow Valley Parkway (#1A) and Lake Minnewanka on the west and south.

The earliest fur-trade route across the Rockies was over Howse Pass. The trail is described in *Life of the Trail 2*, which covers the area bounded by the Kicking Horse River to the south, the Columbia Icefields to the north and the Bow, Mistaya and North Saskatchewan rivers to the east. Later explorers created a popular return trip from the Kootenay Plains by adding an old Native trail down the Amiskwi River to the Howse Pass route. Also included in the volume are the Yoho Valley and the Castleguard Meadows. Today the area is bounded by the Trans-Canada Highway to the south and the Icefields Parkway to the east.

Life of the Trail 3 describes a single route. It follows the Bow River to Bow Pass, then the Mistaya, North Saskatchewan, Sunwapta and Athabasca rivers to the junction with the Miette. Today this is the route of the Trans-Canada Highway and Highway 1A to Lake Louise and the Icefields Parkway north to Jasper. For the sake of clarity, the route has been divided into three sections, presented in the order of first use by non-Aboriginal travellers.

Life of the Trail 4 details the history of three nineteenth-century fur-trade routes and one twentieth-century trail through what is now the southeastern section of Jasper National Park. The area is bounded by the North Saskatchewan River on the south and west, and by the Sunwapta and Athabasca rivers on the west and north. The fur-trade routes of Duncan McGillivray along the Brazeau River and Poboktan Creek, Jacques Cardinal along the southern boundary of Jasper National Park and on into the Job and Coral Creek valleys and Michael Klyne along Maligne

Lake and on into the White Goat Wilderness form the backbone of the trails in the area today. In the 1930s, Fred Brewster developed the Skyline Trail. Today the area is bounded by the David Thompson Highway (#11) in the south, the Icefields Parkway (#93) to the west and the Yellowhead Highway (#16) in the north.

Life of the Trail 5 details the early history of the large area bounded on the north by Lake Minnewanka and the Bow River and on the west by Altrude Creek and the Vermilion and Kootenay rivers. The two main driving forces for excursions into the region were to use White Man, North Kananaskis and Simpson passes to cross the Continental Divide and to find routes leading to Mount Assiniboine. The volume is rounded out with details of the talc mining activity in the Egypt Lakes area. Today the region is bounded by Lake Minnewanka and the Trans-Canada Highway in the north and Highway 93 on the west.

Life of the Trail 6 details historic routes in the large area north of the Columbia Icefields and south of the Miette River, bordered on the east by the Athabasca and Sunwapta rivers (today's Highway 93). The area contains only three historic routes, the most important being the old fur-trade trail over Athabasca Pass. Established by David Thompson in 1811, this trail played a key role in the transcontinental fur trade for nearly 50 years. It became important again towards the end of the nineteenth century as avid mountaineers searched for the supposed giants, Mounts Brown and Hooker. Another historic route leads to Fortress Lake, which was inadvertently discovered by the Coleman brothers as they searched for Mount Brown. The third route, which leads to the spectacular Tonquin Valley, is a twentieth-century route first used by surveyors mapping the Continental Divide.

Life of the Trail 7 delves into the early history of travel in the extensive area north of the Athabasca, Miette and Fraser rivers, or today's Yellowhead Highway (#93). The volume opens with the history of travel along the Yellowhead route, first used by Aboriginal peoples, then by fur traders headed for Tête Jaune Cache. The 1860s saw use by excitement-seekers

Viscount Milton and Walter Cheadle and heavy use by Overlanders en route to the Cariboo gold fields. Late in the nineteenth century the Yellowhead Pass was investigated as a possible route for the Canadian Pacific Railway; later it was used by those railways which later became the Canadian National Railway.

The main interest in the area north of the Fraser River was the towering monarch, Mount Robson. Early mountaineers used Yellowhead Pass in their attempts to reach the base the great mountain. Some followed the Robson River but most pursued the difficult route up the Moose River. Travel to Mount Robson reverted to the Robson River route after Curly Phillips built his famous flying trestle bridge to convey both pedestrians and equestrians to Berg Lake at the base of the mountain.

Mountaineers looking for additional excitement established an alternate route home from Mount Robson by rediscovering and popularizing the old Native route botanists Thomas Drummond and John Alden Loring had followed along the Snake Indian River. Today the Robson River route to Berg Lake is one of the most beautiful and heavily-used routes in the Rockies and the Snake Indian River route (today's North Boundary trail) is a well-maintained trail used by hikers and equestrians seeking peace and quiet in the backcountry.

Whether you share the journey in body or only in mind, the tales in this volume will transport you into the lives of the adventurous souls who have trod these trails. Your imagination will allow you to follow the Overlanders and Milton and Cheadle on their hazardous trips over Yellowhead Pass and along the Fraser River to Tête Jaune Cache. You will join the Coleman brothers and Rev. Kinney on the first trip up the Robson River; the brave can still bush-whack up the Moose River in much the same way as the colourful and efficient Adolphus Moberly did when leading the first mountaineers along the route. And you can participate in the adventures Mary Jobe and her companions and Samuel Prescott Fay undertook in the untracked north country early in the twentieth century.

You will also gain the information you need to follow in their footsteps. Over the years, the authors have hiked many of the trails in this book together. Early in the twenty-first century, Emerson re-hiked each and every one of them in order to provide the most accurate trail information possible. The first person "I" in descriptions of adventures along the trails refers to Emerson and his experiences. We provide a complete trail guide for all routes, including those that do not fall within park boundaries, and have highlighted the trails on a topographic map. Each section begins with a brief overview of the history of that portion of the trail, followed by stories of the known travellers who helped make it what it is today.

We hope that this volume will transport backcountry travellers and armchair adventurers alike into the early days of exploration in this region, so that you will concur with Arthur Conan Doyle when he states:

> I shall hear the roar of rivers where the rapids foam and tear,
> I shall smell the virgin upland with its balsam-laden air,
> And shall dream that I am riding down the winding woody vale,
> With the packer and the packhorse on the Athabaska Trail.[2]

The powerful waterfalls in the Valley of the Thousand Falls create a mystical feeling and sometimes erie sensation in hikers on the Berg Lake trail.

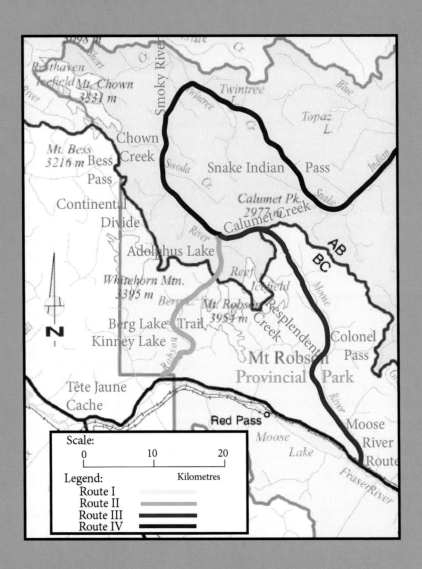

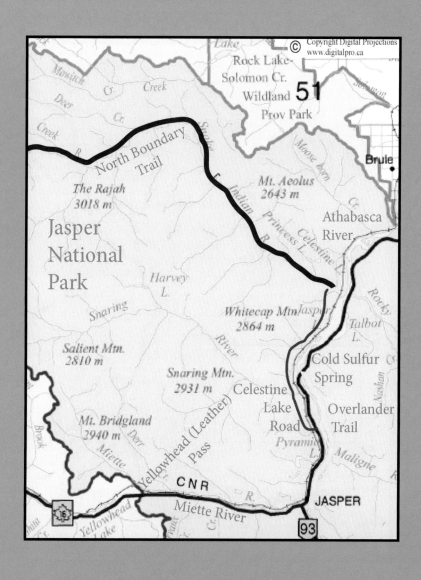

Lake

Rock Lake-
Solomon Cr.
Wildland **51**
Prov Park

Monatch Cr.

Creek

Deer

Cr.

Creek R.

North Boundary
Trail

Smoky R.

Indian R.

Moose horn

Brule

Mt. Aeolus
2643 m

Cr.

The Rajah
3018 m

Princess L.

Celestine L.

Athabasca
River

Jasper
National
Park

Harvey
L.

Whitecap Mtn.
2864 m

Jasper

Rocky

Talbot
L.

Snaring

River

Cold Sulfur
Spring

Cr.

Salient Mtn.
2810 m

Snaring Mtn.
2931 m

Celestine
Lake
Road

Newman

Overlander
Trail

Mt. Bridgland
2940 m

Brook

Deer

Miette

Yellowhead (Leather) Pass

Pyramid
L.

Maligne R.

C N R

R.

JASPER

16

Yellowhead
Lake

Miette River

Cr.

93

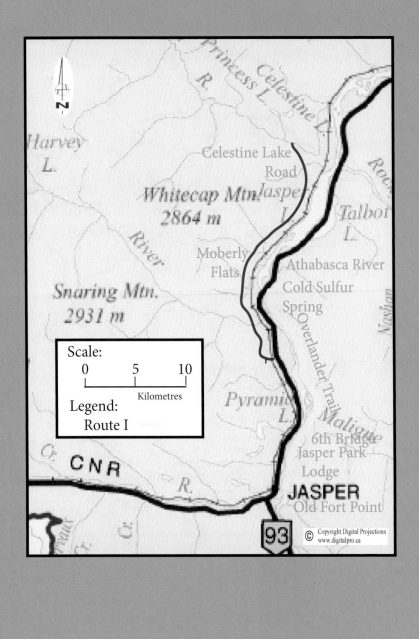

ROUTE I

Leather Pass: From Brûlé Lake to Tête Jaune Cache along the Athabasca,

Miette and Fraser Rivers over Yellowhead Pass (today's Yellowhead Highway)

It was the summer before I turned 64. Over the previous three years I had completed all the hikes on my list except for the very difficult hike up the Moose River to Moose Pass. The latter was not a trail at all, but an important historic route requiring significant route-finding skills. I had intended to complete the hike previously as an adjunct to my 7-day trek along the North Boundary Trail to Mount Robson, but on the advice of hikers I met, I decided to forgo the arduous Moose River portion of the plan and return to the highway via the much easier Berg Lake trail (see Route III below, pages 119-120). However, I could not put it off forever. Reluctant as I was, the time had come to tackle Moose River.

To save my wife Cheryl a lot of driving, I decided to do the trip on my own, using my bicycle to travel between trailheads. I developed an elaborate plan which involved stopping at the Moose River trailhead, hanging my pack from a tree, driving to the Mount Robson Visitor Centre, cycling back to the Moose River trailhead, hiding my bike in the woods, retrieving my pack and hiking the Moose Pass–Berg Lake route back to the Visitor Centre. On my drive home, I would stop and pick up my bike.

Arriving at the Moose River trailhead, I espied a large spruce tree with overhanging branches – the perfect spot to hang my pack out of sight of passing motorists. Although it is often challenging to hang a 25-kilogram pack from a tree without the aid of pulleys, the overhanging branches allowed me to throw a rope and raise the heavy pack without undue difficulty. I then proceeded to the Berg Lake trailhead, where I unloaded my bike and set out for the Moose River trailhead. Fortunately, I had kept my rain suit with me, as the rain that had been threatening all day began in earnest and continued for the entire 35 kilometre uphill bike ride along the road from the Visitor Centre to the trailhead. It was a miserable ride.

Upon arriving at the Moose River trailhead, I noted with satisfaction that my pack was still hanging where I had left it. I quickly surveyed the surroundings to locate a hollow spot in the woods where I could discretely lay the bike on the ground; lock bike, seat and helmet to a tree and cover the lot with a plastic sheet. That task accomplished, I retrieved my pack and started up the Moose River.

Forty-nine hours later I had completed the uphill climb to Moose Pass and on to the junction with the Berg Lake trail, silently chastising myself for listening to the hikers who advised me against attempting to hike the route in two days (see Route III, pages 119-120). Had I ignored their advice and proceeded with my original plan, this entire trip would have been unnecessary. Nevertheless, by late afternoon of the third day I was back at my van. Following my carefully laid plan, I drove to the Moose River trailhead to collect my bike, which had been undisturbed by man or beast, and safely made my way back home.

Chronology

−1800   For thousands of years, Aboriginal peoples travel east from the British Columbia interior through the Yellowhead Pass as part of an indigenous trade network.

1810   Fur trader David Thompson arrives in Jasper to become the first European to visit the area.

1811   The North West Company establishes a post, later known as Jasper House, on Brûlé Lake. Up to 350 horses are kept at the post, which is primarily a supply station for fur brigades crossing the mountains.

     Henry House is built near the confluence of the Miette and Athabasca rivers, near the location of today's Jasper townsite.

1823   A Kamloops-based officer of the Hudson's Bay Company makes the first recorded reference to the Yellowhead Pass.

     Tête Jaune presumably crosses Athabasca Pass to establish his famous cache.

1825   George Simpson instructs Hudson's Bay Company Chief Trader James McMillan to survey the track along the Miette and Fraser rivers between Jasper House and Tête Jaune Cache.

1826   The Hudson's Bay Company sends moose hides and other leather for the New Caledonia district along the Yellowhead Pass route. The pass becomes known as Leather Pass.

1856   Gold is discovered on the Fraser River near its junction with the Thompson River.

1859   James Hector of the Palliser Expedition visits John Moberly at Jasper House and marks the junction of the Miette and Athabasca Rivers on his map.

The first party of Overlanders, led by Pierre C. Pambrun, crosses the Rockies by the Yellowhead Pass route in May.

1861   John Moberly leaves the Hudson's Bay Company. In the fall he persuades a young Métis to accompany him over Yellowhead Pass to Tête Jaune Cache.

1862   Thomas McMicking leads a party of 125 Overlanders and 140 animals from Fort Edmonton to the Yellowhead Pass.

The much smaller 23 man St. Peters party follows slightly more than a week behind the large McMicking party, with the Saskatchewan Gold Expedition close behind.

On September 24 the three Rennie brothers and two friends arrive at Jasper House on a quest for gold. Managing to hire a guide to show them the valley of the Miette, they cross Yellowhead Pass and reach Tête Jaune Cache on October 4.

1863   Viscount Milton and Dr. Cheadle, the first tourists along the Yellowhead Pass route, are attracted by the possibility of finding gold on the Cariboo. They engage the services of Baptiste Supernat, who professes to know the way to Yellowhead Pass and on to Tête Jaune Cache.

The Athabasca River valley from the Overlander trail, looking west, much as the original Overlanders would have seen it.

1864   The British government asks Dr. John Rae to make a hasty trip to investigate the possibility of building a wagon road and telegraph line to connect the colonies in British Columbia to those in central Canada. He proceeds through Jasper, along the Miette River and across Yellowhead Pass to reach Tête Jaune Cache.

1872   Sandford Fleming, engineer-in-chief of the proposed transcontinental railway, orders Walter Moberly to move his survey crew from Howse Pass to the Yellowhead Pass. By the end of the season, the survey has progressed over Yellowhead Pass and east along the Athabasca River.

1878   John Tait, the Kamloops factor for the Hudson's Bay Company, is put in charge of rounding up 425 horses and driving them along the Thompson River towards Tête Jaune Cache and the Yellowhead Pass.

1880   Government surveyors locate a line the railway could take over Yellowhead Pass and along the Thompson River; however, by the end of the year the route is scrapped entirely.

Tom Henderson, his brother Bill and two other young men from New Westminster head east crossing Yellowhead Pass with nine horses, Tom's wife, and six children ranging from eight months to 13 years in age.

1890   Lewis John Swift crosses the Yellowhead Pass for the first time, travelling west from Lac St. Anne to the Okanagan Valley.

1895   Biologist John Alden Loring arrives in Jasper in August to begin a two-year study of the natural history of the Jasper region.

1897   Geologist James McEvoy of the Geological Survey of Canada arrives at the Athabasca River. He continues on to the Miette River and crosses Yellowhead Pass to investigate mines near the pass and Tête Jaune Cache.

1907   Arthur and Lucius Coleman, the Reverend George Kinney and rancher Jack Boker leave Lake Louise for Yellowhead Pass. They cross the pass and reach the Robson River before poor weather and a shortage of supplies turns them back.

Archie McDonald, a mountain man dreaming of a ranch near a beautiful lake in the Cariboo, and his three teenaged sons leave Daysland, Alberta on a hazardous pack-train trip across the Rockies via Yellowhead Pass.

1908   Mary Schäffer, Mollie Adams and their guides Billy Warren and Sid Unwin complete their historic trek to Maligne Lake and then proceed to explore Yellowhead Pass and Tête Jaune Cache.

1909   The Reverend George Kinney heads for Mount Robson with a burning desire to be the first person to climb it. He persuades young guide Curly Phillips to accompany him on the trip over Yellowhead Pass, on to the Moose River and along the river towards Mount Robson.

Guide Fred Stephens embarks on an epic journey from Lacombe, Alberta to the Fraser River with a mining engineer, a cook, his brother Nick as packer and client Stanley Washburn. They cross Yellowhead Pass and proceed to Tête Jaune Cache.

Survey parties for the Grand Trunk Pacific Railway (GTP) select their route as far west as the summit of Yellowhead Pass.

1910   A tote road is built along the GTP right-of-way.

1912   The Grand Trunk Pacific Railway is completed through the Yellowhead Pass.

1913   The Canadian Northern Railway follows.

1914   Novelist Sir Arthur Conan Doyle and his wife Lady Jean visit Jasper. The novelist takes a pack-train trip along the Athabasca and Miette Rivers, over Yellowhead Pass and on to Tête Jaune Cache.

HISTORY

FUR TRADE ERA

In 1810 fur trader David Thompson ventured into the Jasper area, becoming the region's first recorded visitor and setting the stage for the nearly 50-year supremacy of Athabasca Pass as the preferred cross-continental transportation route. Literally thousands of traders and other adventurous souls used the Athabasca River corridor to access Athabasca Pass during that period.[1] Routes along the other two mighty rivers that flow east from the mountains between Mount Robson and the Kananaskis Lakes were no threat to this supremacy. The North Saskatchewan was used for a few years in the early nineteenth century when David Thompson established a fur trade route over Howse Pass, but constant harassment by the Peigan Indians had ended its use by 1811.[2] The Bow River to the south did not rise to prominence until the railway era, when it was made the route of the Canadian Pacific Railway.

The Athabasca River valley in Jasper National Park is a busy transportation corridor with both the Yellowhead Highway and the Canadian National Railway running through it. It has nevertheless managed to retain its beauty, as this image looking south from a vantage point on the Overlander trail makes clear. The highway can be seen on the bottom centre of the image.

Beginning in 1811, fur brigades followed the Athabasca River past its junction with the Miette (just west of today's town of Jasper) to its junction with the Whirlpool River. They would then follow the Whirlpool southwest over Athabasca Pass.

The most hazardous part of the trip along the Athabasca was the diversion around Disaster Point. Cliffs on Roche Miette extended into the Athabasca River and only in the autumn when the river was very low, could travellers ford the river. Historian Richard Wright describes it thus:

> A few rods west of Roche Miette, where the rocky precipice casts a morning shadow on the trail, the Athabasca River runs hard into a rocky ridge and, after a halfhearted attempt at washing it away, veers slightly northward before resuming its eastern flow. The river's erosion had left a steep western face around which the trail must climb, beginning where the river eddied around the face, a place called Disaster Point. From here the trail climbs southward, fenced on the left by timber; on the right is the ever-increasing drop down the steeply angled rock face. ... The rocky path skirted the righthand fall close enough to give vertigo. ... Footsteps became more cautious. Because of the narrowness of the trail, now only a foot wide, the packs rubbed the uphill side and threatened to push the animals over. They climbed to seventeen hundred feet and could plainly see Jasper House below them on the shores of Jasper Lake.[3]

The beckoning (original) Jasper House, so-named for one of the post's early factors, Jasper Hawes, was a North West Company post located on Brûlé Lake at the eastern entrance of today's Jasper National Park.[4] Up to 350 horses were kept there to convey men and supplies into what is now British Columbia.

Farther west, traders would also have passed Henry House. One of David Thompson's men, William Henry, established this post near the confluence of the Miette and Athabasca rivers around 1811 to provide a shelter in which he could spend the winter.[5] Some historians believe that Henry House was built on the site of today's Old Fort Point (near the town of Jasper), and that it was the staging point for brigades travelling over both Yellowhead Pass to posts in present day northern British Columbia and Athabasca Pass, to posts on the Columbia River. In any event, as Jasper House became more important, Henry House gradually fell into disuse.

All nineteenth-century travellers proceeding through the Athabasca River valley faced the unenviable choice of either fording the Athabasca River or climbing the difficult trail over Disaster Point. This 1863 sketch by Dr. Cheadle shows Louis Battenotte, (The Assiniboine), leading a pack horse with the artist urging it to climb the steep trail from behind.

After over a decade as the chief fur trade route through the Rockies, a possible alternative to the supremacy of Athabasca Pass emerged in 1823. That year, a Kamloops-based officer of the Hudson's Bay Company reported that the Shinpoor people who hunted at the head of the North

Thompson River knew of a pass running through both the Cariboo and the Rocky Mountains.[6] That pass, soon known as the Yellowhead, is one of the lowest gaps along the entire length of the Continental Divide.

The origin of the name Yellowhead is uncertain. Some believe it was an Aboriginal nickname for a fair-haired trader – perhaps François Decoigne, who was stationed at Jasper House. Others believe the pass commemorates Pierre Bostonais, an Iroquois trader with blondish hair who was nicknamed Yellowhead. Still others believe the pass was named after Pierre Hatsinaton, an Iroquois known as Tête Jaune, the Yellowhead.[7] Whoever Tête Jaune may have been, he presumably crossed the pass and established his famous cache at the head of navigation of the Fraser River in 1823.

The route was no mystery. Indigenous peoples had been travelling east from the British Columbia interior through the Yellowhead Pass for thousands of years and the fur trade appears to have brought Eastern Aboriginal peoples into the region as well.[8] Evidence from excavations at campsites in the Athabasca River valley indicates an Aboriginal presence near the Snake Indian River as long as 11,000 years ago. Studies at Patricia Lake near the town of Jasper indicate the presence of the Shuswap culture between 4400 and 3200 years ago. By the early nineteenth century, the Beaver people dominated the area and the Cree were becoming increasingly influential. At the same time, other groups – the Ojibwa, Iroquois and Algonquin – were moving west to work for the fur-trading companies and settling along the Yellowhead route between present-day Hinton and Tête Jaune Cache. Early white fur traders and explorers often commented on the number and variety of Aboriginal peoples in this region.[9]

When George Simpson, governor of the newly-merged North West Company and Hudson's Bay Company passed through Jasper in 1825, he instructed chief trader James McMillan to survey the track between Jasper House and Tête Jaune Cache.[10] The survey, carried out later that year, ran from Jasper House to Henry House, over Yellowhead Pass, past Yellowhead Lake and Moose Lake and along the banks of the Fraser

River to Tête Jaune Cache. In his report to William Connolly of Fort St. James, McMillan reported that "with very little trouble horses will pass their loads with ease."[11]

In 1826 it was resolved that moose hides and other dressed leather needed by traders in the New Caledonia district to make tents, moccasins and other items such as pack cords should be sent via the Yellowhead Pass route. From 1826 to 1830 the brigades split at the mouth of the Miette, with part of the brigade continuing west over Athabasca Pass and the remainder continuing north over Yellowhead Pass or "Leather Pass," as it became known. But the challenge to the dominance of Athabasca Pass did not last long. Although Yellowhead Pass was indeed as easy to navigate as McMillan reported, the same could not be said of the Fraser River and the route was soon abandoned.

The Parting of the Brigades 1826 by Walter J. Phillips illustrates the Yellowhead Pass group of the westbound Hudson's Bay Company brigade continuing west along the Miette (with Pyramid Mountain in the background) and the Athabasca Pass group fording the Miette River en route to the Whirlpool.

Although early travellers were well-aware of the Yellowhead route, most preferred to use Athabasca Pass and few saw reason to continue along the Miette to Yellowhead Pass. For instance, when the Palliser Expedition's James Hector visited John Moberly at Jasper House in 1859, he marked the junction of the Miette and Athabasca rivers on his map but refrained from exploring further along the Miette. The exception was former HBC factor John Moberly. After having left the Hudson's Bay Company in the fall of 1861, Moberly persuaded a young Métis to accompany him over Yellowhead Pass to Tête Jaune Cache. Deep snow meant that even the Yellowhead was difficult to cross, and they had to spend considerable time cutting through fallen timber and brush on the trail. Nevertheless, they succeeded in reaching the Cache in six days and continued down the Fraser River by canoe.[12]

THE ALLURE OF GOLD

The Overlanders are by far the best-known early travellers who crossed the Yellowhead Pass. Drawn by dreams of instant wealth, these adventurers were lured from eastern Canada by misleading advertising promising easy access to the gold fields by way of a well-used route across the Rockies to the Fraser River. Pierre C. Pambrun led the first party over the Yellowhead Pass route in May of 1859. Other members of the group were Ned Hine, Brewster, John R. Sanford, C.D. Loveland, E.W.W. Linton and Alfred Perry. Little is known about their trip over the pass and down the Fraser except that on July 19, a clerk at the Hudson's Bay Company post at Fort Edmonton mater-of-factly noted: "Three of the Yankees who left this place with P.C. Pambrun for New Caledonia returned from Jaspers. They say I guess it's no go."[13]

Exploration and prospecting continued all along the Fraser River in 1860. The season's most noteworthy prospector was Timoleon M. Love, a gunsmith by apprentice, house carpenter by trade and adventurer by nature whose true passion was seeking gold.[14] While working along the Fraser in 1860, Love formed an eastbound prospecting party with four other miners. They travelled over the Yellowhead Pass and on to Jasper House, which clerk Henry Moberly had just re-opened. Love's party split up at Jasper House to prospect as much of the country as possible.

Overlanders (1858–1862)

Gold! Gold on Fraser's River! The news spread like wildfire drawing hopeful thousands from all directions motivated by dreams of instant wealth. No one knows the actual numbers, the extent of their hardships or how many lost their lives, but some historians argue that this was the largest movement of men to a particular location in such a short space of time. Up to 30,000 came from the west coast of North America, with a smaller but still significant number coming from the eastern side of the continent. Those who travelled to the interior of British Columbia by land soon became known as the Overlanders.

The rush began as a trickle in 1858; of the 86 adventurers who began the journey that season, not one reached the Fraser River gold fields – though with great difficulty a party of ten did manage to cross the mountains by a southerly pass.[15] The activity increased the following year; at one time at least ten parties were scattered across the plains from St. Paul in Minnesota to Fort Edmonton in the northwest. Only one of these managed to cross the Rockies via the Yellowhead pass, though others crossed by a more southerly route. In 1861, another small party managed to cross the Continental Divide over Vermilion Pass, south of the Bow River.

News that the Fraser gold rush was a "humbug" had travelled east late in 1858. Then gold was discovered on the Quesnel River and news of the nearby strike in an area called the Cariboo started to trickle in. News of a rich strike in the Cariboo was confirmed in 1861; the following year the real migration of Overlanders began. The most common route was through American territory to St. Paul, then north to Fort Garry using whatever form of transportation was available. From Fort Garry, most took the Carlton Trail to Fort Edmonton, travelling in large groups by horseback and Red River cart.

In 1862, a large number of small parties formed in Ontario and from further east headed for St. Paul, with the size of each party fluctuating as some members departed and others joined. Considerable consolidation took place as they neared Fort Garry, resulting in three large parties consisting of 250 men and four women. The largest of these was the McMicking party, known for the efficiency and integrity of its leader. The smallest was a party of Americans, with the Saskatchewan Gold Expedition of intermediate size.

Most of the Overlanders were men from eastern Canada and the United States seeking wealth and fame in the gold fields of the Cariboo. Thomas McMicking, leader of one of the largest parties to cross the continent, was known for his exceptional efficiency and integrity.

One remarkable group to join the McMicking party was the Schubert family, consisting of Augustus, Catherine and their three children. Unknown to the leaders was the fact that

Catherine was pregnant at the time they joined the group. Although much has been made of a pregnant woman walking across the plains, Catherine Schubert was unique in the fact that she was a white woman of Anglo-Saxon descent. Several children had been born during the original "overland" trips from Fort Garry to the mouth of the Columbia River led by James Sinclair in 1841 and 1854.[16] However, these were all Métis women for whom giving birth on the trail was not considered unusual. Of the four women who joined the 1862 Overlanders, three were Métis and nothing is known about their travels. The men who kept diaries of their journeys simply did not mention them.

Francis Augustus Schubert was a member of the large McMicking party of Overlanders that crossed Yellowhead Pass en route to Tête Jaune Cache and the gold fields of the Cariboo. He was exceptional only in that his wife and three children accompanied him on this ambitious journey.

The three parties overcame extreme fatigue of people and animals, disagreements and disputes, quarrels and fights, fear and anticipation to reach Fort Edmonton where final decisions on participation, routes and passes had to be made. The McMicking party was reduced to 125 men and 140 animals; the American party, now known as the St. Peters party, to 23 men and the Saskatchewan Gold party to approximately 32, half of its original size. All proceeded west towards Tête Jaune Cache, and as the mountains came into sight men were moved to write poetry, quote scripture and write passionate letters home. Little did they realize that the closer they drew to paradise, the more difficult the trek was to become. Thoughts soon turned to more practical concerns of how to prevent starvation and scurvy.[17]

When they reached Tête Jaune Cache late that August and early in September, the last big decision had to be made: whether to try to cut a path overland to the Cariboo, press overland to the headwaters of the Thompson River or take the shortest and most dangerous route down the Fraser. Groups reconfigured based on the route of choice. Approximately 40 adventurers chose the Thompson route; of those, two drowned en route. Those who rafted down the Fraser suffered no loss of life; four of those who attempted the Fraser in dugout canoes died along the way. All suffered great hardship.

Catherine Schubert crossed the continent with her husband and three children as part of the McMicking party of Overlanders. Unknown to the group, she was pregnant at the time and soon after they arrived at Fort Kamloops gave birth to the first white child in central British Columbia. Though Métis women often travelled while pregnant and gave birth on the trail, it was unusual for a white woman to do so.

As a gold-seeking expedition, the Overlanders' trek was a total failure. The few prospectors who did reach the Cariboo and attempted to mine found that the gold deposits had been nearly exhausted by earlier arrivals. Nevertheless, the initiative did have positive results. The approximately 200 Overlanders who passed through the Rocky Mountains in 1862 helped demonstrate that land barriers to the union of British Columbia with eastern Canada could be overcome.

Even more significant was the profound effect the adventurers had on the development of British Columbia. Many stayed and began businesses on the coast or settled the interior. Others turned their talents to civic development and were instrumental in the introduction of telegraph, telephone and electric power into the province. Together, they became part of the heritage of the province of British Columbia, which has benefitted tremendously from the self-sufficiency and organizational capacity they developed on the long and arduous journey west.

Although little prospecting appears to have been accomplished, Love nonetheless sent out glowing reports of gold discoveries near Fort Edmonton on the North Saskatchewan River. Doubtless many of the Overlanders who chose to proceed west from Edmonton over the Yellowhead Pass would have chosen the easier, but longer, southern passes had they not been influenced by Love's reports.[18]

One such party, the Thomas McMicking party, consisted of 125 people and 140 animals. Having consulted with several HBC fur traders and freemen at Fort Edmonton regarding the best route through the mountains, McMicking reported:

All parties ... agreed that the Boundary, Cootanie and Sinclair [Kananaskis] Passes were the easiest and presented the fewest difficulties; but recommended the Leather, Cow-Dung Lake, or Jasper Pass [all the Yellowhead now] for our purpose, as being the shortest and most direct way to Cariboo; altho' some of them represented the road as nearly impassable, and foresaw difficulties and dangers which they considered almost insurmountable. After thoroughly examining the matter, and carefully comparing notes we decided to try the Leather Pass.[19]

André Cardinal, a member of a large Métis family living in the St. Albert–Lac St. Anne area, who had considerable experience with the Yellowhead Pass route to Tête Jaune Cache, was chosen as guide. The men busily traded oxen and carts for horses and pack-saddles in preparation for the trip to the mountains. On Tuesday July 29, 1862 they headed north for St. Albert. Two weeks later, McMicking revealed:

On Wednesday, [August] the 13th, precisely at 12 o'clock noon, as the train emerged from a thick spruce swamp...we obtained the first distinct view of the Rocky Mountains. Although we were yet one hundred miles from them, their dark outline was plainly visible far above the level of the horizon, and their lofty snowclad peaks, standing out in bold relief against the blue sky beyond, and glistening in the sunlight, gave them the appearance of fleecy clouds floating in the distance. The company were enraptured at the sight of them; for whatever dangers or difficulties might possibly be in store for us among them, all were heartily tired of the endless succession of hills and streams and swamps and swamps and streams and hills and were willing to face almost any danger that would be likely to terminate or vary our toils.[20]

As the party moved deeper into the mountains, the enclosing landscape brought depression to some of the men who were used to the open horizons of the plains. One man, James Sellar, was thinking of his wife whom he left behind and on a lonely day was prompted to pen these lines:

> When we two parted
>
> In silence & tears,
>
> To sever for years,
>
> Pale grew thy cheek, & cold,
>
> Colder thy kiss,
>
> How true that moment foretold
>
> Trails like this![21]

They camped one night below the sheer cliffs and towering columns of Roche Miette and the following day made the 1700-foot (518 metre) ascent over Disaster Point before dropping steeply down to the Rocky River ford.

The morning of the 20th saw them fording to the west side of the downstream of the Maligne River and camping at what Cardinal told them was the site of Old Fort Henry.[22] Two days later, they turned up the Miette towards the pass. Fallen timber and repeated fords slowed their progress considerably. Nevertheless, by four o'clock that afternoon they had crossed the Continental Divide to attain the headwaters of the Fraser River. The pleasure of this accomplishment was muted by the extensive chopping that was required along Yellowhead Lake, the north side of the Fraser River and Moose Lake. Progress was excruciatingly slow, food was in short supply and oxen had to be killed as pemmican ran out.

On August 27 McMicking wrote: "We were aroused from our slumbers on Wednesday morning by our guide shouting through the camp, 'Hurrah! For Tête Jaune Cache,' and were informed that we should reach the Cache, if not misfortune befel us, some time during the day."[23] They arrived at 4:14 pm.

The excitement of arriving at the Cache was tempered by the decisions that had to be made. There were three main choices: to cut a trail across the Premier Range to the Cariboo, to continue overland to the headwaters of the Thompson and follow it to Fort Kamloops, or to attempt the Fraser, the shortest and most dangerous route. The groups were reconfigured based on which route each individual or family preferred. A group of 36 drove 130 animals along the lengthy Thompson route while the remaining 84 followed the Fraser River. Although most made it through the mountains, hardly any continued on to the Cariboo. Their adventures to date had been so gruelling that they felt it best to seek work along the coast.

Tête Jaune Cache was located at a natural crossroads – the head of navigation for the Fraser River – and played a major role in the construction of the Canadian Northern and Grand Trunk Pacific railroads early in the twentieth century. This 1911 image shows it as a booming frontier town, very different from the 1860s when it was little more than a name with a few shacks. The original site is now submerged by the Fraser River.

The dust from the McMicking party had barely settled when the next party of Overlanders arrived at Fort Edmonton. The St. Peters party was much smaller, consisting of 21 easterners plus two who had been picked up en route at Lac St. Anne (67 km west of Fort Edmonton). Slightly more than a week behind the large McMicking party, the men headed west "along the terrible swampy road that the McMicking party had churned into a quagmire."[24] Like that of the previous party, "their journey was a succession of bogs, windfall, and river crossings that kept the men muddy and wet. Provisions ran low and the men were hungry."[25] They reached the Cache on September 8 to find that many men from previous parties were still there, preparing for the next stage of their journey.

The self-branded Saskatchewan Gold Expedition was close on their heels. On August 12, after only four days at Fort Edmonton, half of the group decided to winter in the area. The remainder headed west. They reached the Athabasca River on September 4 and sent six men ahead to the Cache to start building canoes. Sickness and starvation forced the advance party to stop at Moose Lake, where they waited for the main party. The combined party overcame injury, illness and exhaustion to reach Tête Jaune Cache on September 16. They promptly set to work building canoes for the trip down the Fraser.

Despite the lateness of the season, they were not the last of the Overlanders to cross Yellowhead Pass in 1862. The Rennie party of five men – three Rennie brothers and two others – arrived at Jasper House on September 24. They avoided Disaster Point by crossing the Athabasca on a raft and managed to hire a guide at Jasper House to lead them to the valley of the Miette. They successfully crossed Yellowhead Pass to reach Tête Jaune Cache, which they described as an old deserted station of the HBC, on October 4.

Faced with deciding which river to take and whether to attempt it on a raft or a canoe, they chose canoes on the Fraser. Little did they know how dreadful the outcome would be. Only two made it to Fort George; the three who were too weak to travel died of hypothermia and starvation – despite having resorted to cannibalism – when the two surviving brothers were unable to rescue them. They were not alone in their failure; there is no evidence that any of the Overlanders ever found the fortune they so ardently sought. Most of those who managed to make it through the mountains alive did, however, remain in British Columbia, swelling the population of this fledgling colony.

THE FIRST TOURISTS

The surge of Overlanders in the fall of 1862 brought more visitors to Tête Jaune Cache than it had seen for the previous 100 years or was to see for the next 50. However, a taste of things to come arrived the following spring in the form of the first tourists to cross Yellowhead Pass. Not unlike the Earl of Southesk on his 1859 journey to the eastern Rockies, Viscount Milton and Dr. Walter Cheadle were seeking adventure hunting buffalo and grizzlies.[26] They also, truth be told, had their sights on the gold of the Cariboo. In April, 1863 at Fort Carlton, they engaged the services of Baptiste Supernat, who professed to know the way to Yellowhead Pass and on to Tête Jaune Cache. Later that spring, they met Louis Battenotte, known as "The Assiniboine," at Fort Pitt. Anxious to cross the mountains with his wife and son, Battenotte offered to accompany them. Finally, at Fort Edmonton, they were coerced into allowing Mr. O'Beirne, a notorious ne'er do well, to accompany them. According to Milton and Cheadle:

Mr. O'B. was an Irishman of between forty and fifty years of age, of middle height and wiry make. His face was long and its features large, and a retreating mouth, almost destitute of teeth, gave a greater prominence to his rather elongated nose. He was dressed in a long coat of alpaca, of ecclesiastical cut, and wore a black wide-awake, which ill accorded with the week's stubble on his chin, fustian trousers, and highlows tied with string. He carried an enormous stick, and altogether his appearance showed a curious mixture of the clerical with the rustic. His speech was rich with the brogue of his Native isle, and his discourse ornamented with numerous quotations from the ancient classics.... After holding out several days, we were overcome by his importunity, and agreed that he should form one of our party, in spite of the rebellious grumbling of Baptiste and The Assiniboine. Mr. O'B. thanked us, but assured us that we had in reality acted for our own interest, and congratulated us upon having decided so wisely, for he should be very useful, and ask no wages.[27]

Eugene Francis O'Beirne (sometimes spelled O'Byrne) (c. 1809–11–sometime after 1865)

Eugene Francis O'Beirne, known as Mr. O'B, was born to farmers John and Claire O'Beirne in Newtown Forbes, County Longford, Republic of Ireland, circa 1809–1811. He attended St. Patrick's Roman Catholic theological college at Maynooth, County Kildare between 1826 and 1830 but was expelled before graduation and ordination to the priesthood. Four years later he enrolled in Trinity College, Dublin but appears to have spent most of his time working on two pamphlets attacking the College of Maynooth (*Maynooth in 1834* and *A Succinct and Accurate Account of the System of Discipline, Education and Theology Adopted and Pursued in the Popish College of Maynooth (1840)*). He subsequently became an apostate, spending the years between 1836 and 1839 on an anti-Catholic lecture tour of England that emphasized his assessment of the College of Maynooth as a den of filth and iniquity. At times his comments became so offensive his audience forced him to terminate his lecture.

In 1842 he was admitted to St. John's College, Cambridge but after five months was encouraged to transfer to Clare College, from which he was removed 18 months later without obtaining a degree. His activities and whereabouts for the next 18 years are somewhat obscure. It is believed that he spent a year or two in India before making his way to Louisiana, USA. After the outbreak of civil war in the late 1850s he moved north. In 1861 he attempted to obtain ordination in the Episcopal Church in Minnesota or, failing that, a teaching position. His attempts must have been unsuccessful on both counts as he ended up in the Red River Settlement in September of that year.

Mr. O'Beirne, the ne'er do well parasite who attached himself to the Milton and Cheadle party to cross the mountains in 1863, was deathly afraid of mounting a horse – even in order to cross deep rushing rivers. This sketch by Dr. Cheadle shows how he used the tail of Cheadle's horse Bucephalus to maintain his balance on the treacherous crossing.

Though initially regarded as somewhat of a celebrity, he soon developed a reputation as a scrounger and inevitably outlived his welcome. In the spring of 1862 Bishop Anderson presented O'Beirne with sufficient funds to travel as far as Canada (Ontario). He set out towards Pembina, wasting no time in squandering the bishop's funding and losing favour with the leaders at Pembina. Much to the dismay of the people at Red River, he returned in the spring.

Realizing he was unwelcome in that community, O'Beirne managed to attach himself to a group of Overlanders heading west to the gold fields of the Cariboo. By the time they reached Fort Carlton, they were thoroughly fed up with his selfishness, impudence, egotism, indolence and dishonesty and left him there to fend for himself. He managed to procure passage to Fort Edmonton on one of the Hudson's Bay Company boats and spent the winter with pioneer Methodist missionaries Thomas Woolsey and John McDougall. By March of 1863, they could stand him no longer and McDougall brought him to Fort Edmonton.

O'Beirne managed to survive the next two months in a small shack on the banks of the North Saskatchewan River. In May, two adventurous English travellers, Viscount Milton and Dr. Walter Cheadle, arrived at the Fort and O'Beirne set out to convince them to take him with them on their journey through the mountains. Against their better judgment, they agreed. In early June, they departed on a long and extremely difficult trip to Tête Jaune Cache and down the Thompson River to Kamloops, where they arrived in September, exhausted and starving. O'Beirne had proven to be a helpless, quarrelsome, uncooperative and extremely timid companion.

At Kamloops O'Beirne was given some supplies and arrangements were made for him to proceed alone to Victoria. There he attempted to rebuild his faith under the tutelage of the local clergy. However, he soon left for San Francisco, where he boarded a ship bound for Melbourne, Australia. He arrived in

January 1864 and apparently continued his career as a peripatetic pedagogue and philosopher before disappearing from history. No record of his death has been uncovered.

O'Beirne was not an outdoorsman in any sense of the word and it is hard to imagine a more unlikely character travelling across the Canadian west in the 1860s. He was obviously very intelligent and could provide endless scholarly quotes in Latin. His favourite pastime was sitting out of sight under a tree reading from Paley's *Evidences of Christianity* while others worked. Under different circumstances he might have become a lecturer at one of the leading educational institutions in England; however, his personality was such that it is hard to imagine him succeeding at anything. Nevertheless, he has become a significant part of the folklore of the Rocky Mountains and in 1918 surveyor Arthur Wheeler chose to name Mount O'Beirne on the Alberta–British Columbia boundary in his honour. Significantly, neither Viscount Milton nor Dr. Cheadle chose to immortalize O'Beirne's name in the mountains, although they did name mountains after one another.

Milton and Cheadle intended to explore the gold fields of the Cariboo, which meant taking the Yellowhead Pass. Because the fur brigades coming over Athabasca Pass from the Columbia River had not yet relayed information on the ultimate fate of the Overlanders of 1862, very little information was available on the route beyond Tête Jaune Cache. Enough was known however, for those at Fort Edmonton to encourage travellers to chose an alternative route. According to Milton and Cheadle:

Mr. Hardisty, and the other officers of the Fort, tried earnestly to dissuade us from attempting to cross by the Leather Pass, alleging that the season was not yet far enough advanced, and the rivers would be at their height, swollen by the melting of the mountain snows. They assured us that many of the streams were fierce and rocky torrents, exceedingly dangerous to cross, except when low in the autumn, and that the country on the west of the mountains, as far as it was known, was a region rugged and inhospitable, everywhere covered with impenetrable forest; and even if we descended the Fraser, instead of attempting to reach Cariboo, we should find that river full of rapids and whirlpools, which had often proved fatal to the most expert canoemen. This pass...had been formerly used by the voyageurs of the Hudson's Bay Company as a portage from the Athabasca to the Fraser, but had long been abandoned on account of the numerous casualties which attended the navigation of the latter river.[28]

One of the most unlikely groups to cross the mountains from Fort Edmonton to Fort Victoria in the mid 1800s was made up of Viscount Lord Milton and his personal physician and friend Dr. Walter Cheadle. The pair, guided by Louis Battenotte (The Assiniboine), was exploring the country with no specific objective. The entire party, shown here, consisted of: (l–r) Mrs. Battenotte, Louis Battenotte (The Assiniboine), Dr. Walter Cheadle, Viscount Lord Milton and the Battonette's son Baptiste.

Nevertheless, the gentlemen were determined to follow their original plan, tracing the Overlanders' path as far as Tête Jaune Cache and then trusting "to our imperfect maps and the sagacity of our men, to reach either Cariboo or Fort Kamloops at the grand fork of the Thompson, as circumstances might render advisable."[29]

By June 3, 1863 the motley party consisting of Milton, Cheadle, Mr. O'B., Baptiste Supernat, The Assiniboine, his wife (commonly called Mrs. Assiniboine) and their 13-year-old son, was ready to depart for the mountains. They had 13 horses, six of which carried packs, and a 50-day supply of provisions. Not long thereafter, Baptiste Supernat deserted the party, taking one of their best horses. The Assiniboine was promoted to the position of guide. In spite of an earlier injury which had left only two fingers on one hand, he performed this new role admirably. It is to his credit that the party completed their journey without any loss of life. He ably led them across the prairie, into the mountains and past the treacherous cliffs around Roche Miette. Near Jasper House, the party began constructing a raft upon which to cross the Athabasca River. A local Métis saved them from completing the task by pointing out a safe ford and also assisted them in engaging the services of an old Iroquois Métis to accompany them as far as Tête Jaune Cache in return for a pack horse. He did not know anything of the country beyond the Cache and would go no further.

William Wentworth-Fitzwilliam, Viscount Milton (1839–1877)

William Wentworth-Fitzwilliam was born on July 27, 1839 in London, England, the eldest son of William Thomas Spenser Wentworth-Fitzwilliam, 6th Earl of Fitzwilliam, and Francis Harriet Douglas. As eldest son he stood to inherit the massive family fortune and the title of Earl of Fitzwilliam. Following in the path of the English elite, he was educated at Eton College and Trinity College, Cambridge.

He was a good student, sensitive and romantic, but always in poor health. Early family history does not give any indication as to what his health problems were, but his great-great-grandson, Michael Shaw Bond, concludes from rather convincing evidence that Milton was epileptic.[30] Epilepsy was not accepted by nineteenth century society and the fact that most people would have thought of him as freakish, mentally unbalanced, anti-social or simply mad would have been difficult for Milton to bear. Sadly, the aristocracy was particularly adverse to acknowledging such health conditions, and it seems that Milton's family and friends were no more accepting than the broader community.

In 1859 the Earl of Southesk, who was a friend of Milton's father, had crossed the Canadian prairies and travelled in the Rocky Mountains.[31] It is likely stories of this trip that prompted Milton, an avid horseman, to take a trip to Red River (today's Manitoba) in 1860 to hunt buffalo. The trip freed Milton from the stigma that he had to bear at home; life in the wild seemed to suit him.

In 1861, an announcement of Milton's forthcoming marriage to Miss Dorcas Chichester appeared, only to be quickly retracted. The reason given was that Milton had been misinformed about the age of his prospective bride. Bond feels that this was a fantastic excuse, the marriage of a 22-year-old to a 17-year-old not being at all uncommon, and surmises that the family forbade the marriage because of Milton's epilepsy.

Less than a year after breaking off his engagement to Dorcas Chichester, Milton left England for Canada with the intention of travelling across the prairies and through the mountains to

Viscount Lord Milton was the eldest son of the
6th Earl of Fitzwilliam and as such, was in line
to inherit his father's title and massive fortune.
Lord Milton was epileptic, however, a condition
which was not accepted by upper-class Britons of
the time. Milton's trip across Canada was likely
predicated on a desire to escape the societal
stigma he faced.

the gold fields of the Cariboo. He considered himself fortunate to obtain the assistance of a friend, Dr. Walter Butler Cheadle, who turned out to be the real leader of the expedition. As an epileptic, it was a great advantage for Milton to travel with a personal physician, but not once during all of his time in the wild did Milton suffer an epileptic attack; the first occurred when the duo reached civilization at Victoria.

In the Caribou, Milton and Cheadle had honoured one another by naming Mount Milton and Mount Cheadle. Back on the coast, Milton prepared for an eventual return by purchasing seven small lots in New Westminster, southeast of Vancouver. He and Cheadle left Victoria in December 1863, visiting San Francisco, Panama and New York en route to England. Almost immediately after their return in March of 1864, Milton left on a nation-wide lecture tour, entrancing his audiences with stories of his travels.

The account he and Cheadle published of their journey, *The North-West Passage by Land 1865* (London: Cassell, Petter and Galpin, 1865), met with immediate success. Although Milton's name appears first on the book title page, subsequent comparison of the book to Cheadle's diary makes it clear that most of the writing was his.

After returning to England, Milton carried on the family tradition of entering politics, winning a seat as member of Parliament for Yorkshire in 1865. Although he held the seat until 1872, unlike his father, he did not excel in the role of parliamentarian and was most interested when questions regarding the Red River Settlement and the colony of British Columbia came up in the House. In 1869, while still an MP, Milton published and paid for *A History of the San Juan water boundary dispute question as affecting the division of territory between Great Britain and the United States* (London and New York, 1869).

In August 1867 Lord Milton married Laura Maria Theresa Beauclerk, daughter of Lord Charles Beauclerk, in London. Five years later, after resigning his seat in Parliament, Milton took his pregnant wife and two daughters and left England for good, probably realizing that an epileptic could not make a life for himself there. The family first lived in a farmhouse in Pointe de Meuron, near where the reconstructed Fort William stands today. There their son, who would in due course inherit the title of his grandfather, was born. Within a year the farmhouse burned down and Milton took his family to an equally remote spot near Richmond, Virginia, where their fourth child was born. Nothing is known about Milton's time in Virginia; the family may have lived under an assumed name.

Lord Milton died on January 17, 1877 in Rouen, France. There is no record of why he was there or of how he died (nor of what happened to the land he had purchased in New Westminster). He was buried at Wentworth in the Fitzwilliam family mausoleum. Since he predeceased his father, he did not inherit the title of Earl of Fitzwilliam. Laura continued to live in Virginia for some time after his death and left her Virginia house to two of her sisters. She died ten years after her husband, also at the age of 37, and was buried beside him at Wentworth, although it seems likely that both would have preferred a hilltop grave somewhere in the North American wilderness.

The final family insult to Lord Milton came when Milton's brothers, who were living at Wentworth with his son Billy, the lawful heir to the Fitzwilliam earldom, contested his eligibility, claiming that he was not the son of Lord Milton. The case was dropped and Lord Milton's son became the 7th Earl of Fitzwilliam on the death of his grandfather. It seems that only in death was Lord Milton absolved by his family. The epitaph on his tomb reads:

> Fear not: for I have redeemed thee,
> I have called thee by thy name;
> Thou art mine. (Isaiah 43:1)

They headed out again on July 4, with The Assiniboine back in the lead. They continued past the site of old Henry House and on up the valley of the Miette River:

The track, leaving the valley of the Athabasca at this point, turned towards the north-west, and entered a narrow rocky ravine, the valley of the river Myette [sic]. The stream was not more than thirty yards in width, but deep and rapid, and its bed beset with great rocks and boulders. The path was obstructed by large stones and fallen timber, lying so thickly that our two men were kept hard at work all the afternoon, and the horses progressed only by a succession of jumps…At mid-day we reached the place where we were to cross the river, and pulled up to make a raft. After crossing by this means, we toiled on through a ravine so narrow, and where the mountains came down so close to the water's edge, that, in order to pass them we were compelled to traverse the stream no less than six times more before evening. In each of these cases we crossed on horseback, the river now being a succession of rapids, not more than four or five feet deep. These passages of the river were difficult, and many of them dangerous, for the water was very high, and the current extremely powerful....

[T]he fifth day after leaving Jasper House, and in the course of our morning's journey we were surprised by coming upon a stream flowing to the westward. We had unconsciously passed the height of land and gained the watershed of the Pacific. The ascent had been so gradual and imperceptible, that, until we had the evidence of the water flow, we had no suspicion that we were even near the dividing ridge...On the 10th we struck the Fraser River, sweeping round from the south-west through a narrow gorge, to expand some miles lower down into Moose Lake.[32]

They reached Moose Lake by noon on July 11 and were most impressed by the topography. They describe the scenery as "very wild and grand," explaining that "On the south side, the hills rose perpendicularly out of the water for perhaps 2,000 feet, beyond which was the usual background of rocky and hoary peaks. Over the edge of this mighty precipice a row of silver streams poured with unbroken fall, the smaller one [sic] dissipated in mist and spray ere they reached the lake below. This beautiful series of cascades we named the Rockingham Falls."[33] Unable to find a suitable resting place before dark, they were forced to spend the night in a sand pit, with no feed for the horses.

Their difficulties continued as they proceeded along the route towards Tête Jaune Cache. Two pack horses, only one of which was recovered, were swept away in the flood-swollen river. The party was left with:

neither tea, salt, nor tobacco, for our whole store of these luxuries had been carried by the horse which was lost. All our clothes, matches, and ammunition were gone, except what we carried on our persons at the time. All our papers, letters of credit, and valuables, Milton's buffalo robe and blanket, Cheadle's collection of plants, the instruments and watches, had set out on their voyage towards the sea. But there was much reason for congratulation as well as lamentation. No actual necessaries of life had gone; we had still the pemmican and flour. The journals, too,…were saved.[34]

They successfully attained Tête Jaune Cache on July 17, little realizing that the biggest challenges of the journey were yet to come. Though they did manage to gradually make their way to the Thompson River, they arrived in very poor shape with very little food. Any hope of reaching the Cariboo having been extinguished, they headed overland for Fort Kamloops. They struggled on for five weeks, killing horses for food, until they eventually reached Fort Kamloops exhausted and starving.

Above: This sketch by Dr. Cheadle illustrates one of many instances when Louis Battenotte (The Assiniboine) made a heroic effort to save the party from grief. He plunged into the dangerous rapid to grab the horse and help it to safety. The other horse in the sketch, together with the pack containing valuable necessities, was irretrievably lost.

Opposite: Dr. John Rae, a Hudson's Bay Company doctor, established a reputation for efficient northern travel during his Arctic search for the lost Franklin expedition. As a result, he was chosen to locate a possible wagon road and telegraph line to connect the West Coast with central Canada.

TRAIL FINDERS

Although Yellowhead Pass was soon abandoned by the fur trade, it continued to be included in a transcontinental transportation system. The year after Viscount Milton and Dr. Cheadle passed through, the pass was crossed by an entirely different type of traveller interested in neither furs, nor gold, nor pure adventure.

Dr. John Rae had been selected by the Hudson's Bay Company, the British and Canadian governments and the Grand Trunk Railway to investigate a possible wagon road and telegraph line that would connect the colonies in British Columbia to central Canada.[35] Rae had established a reputation as an accomplished traveller a decade earlier during his 1853–54 search through the Arctic for the ill-fated Franklin expedition. He now set off to traverse the prairies and cross the mountains to the West Coast.

Rae's party left Fort Garry (Winnipeg) on June 25, 1864. He and his men managed to cross the prairies and foothills, circumnavigate Disaster Point without climbing, proceed along the Miette River and across Yellowhead Pass to Tête Jaune Cache – a distance of over 400 miles (644 km) – in less than a month. They then descended the Fraser River to Fort George at its mouth in a dugout canoe obtained at Tête Jaune Cache.

Although Rae spoke favourably about the feasibility of building a telegraph line, the project never went forward. Yellowhead Pass was left in its natural state – for the time being. But concern for cross-continental transportation had not abated. Decision-makers in the emergent Dominion of Canada had simply turned their attention to building a railway from coast to coast. In the spring of 1871, Prime Minister John A. MacDonald appointed Sandford Fleming as engineer-in-chief of the proposed transcontinental railway. Fleming dispatched 21 survey parties throughout the West to begin the monumental task of determining a route for the railway.

Meanwhile, the first attempt at a geological survey of the Yellowhead Pass was getting underway. Chief Dominion Geologist Alfred R.C. Selwyn, his assistant and photographers Benjamin Baltzly and John Hammond, had an extremely difficult passage east through the North Thompson River valley.[36] Selwyn reported that "the obstructions encountered in penetrating the dense and pathless forest and jungle which prevail almost unbroken, except by swamps and rivers, for more that 150 miles on the line of route travelled from Kamloops to the Leather [Yellowhead] Pass in the Rocky Mountains."[37]

They had planned to meet a survey crew near present-day Valemount, southwest of the Fraser River and Yellowhead Pass, but the crew was nowhere to be found and Selwyn's pack horses had been pushed to their limit. He sent most of the horses back to Kamloops while he, packer McLennan, Baltzly and some guides pushed on towards Leather Pass. Five days of difficult travel got the exhausted party past Moose Lake on the Fraser River, but not to Cowdung (Yellowhead) Lake and the pass.

Concerned about the very real risk of becoming trapped in the mountains for the winter, they decided to retreat. Of the 150 horses and mules in the original pack train, only 26 made it back to Kamloops. Some died from cold, hunger and overwork in the near-impassable country; most were simply abandoned or perished in snowstorms.[38]

When the federal government decided to build a railroad to connect the new province of British Columbia to the eastern provinces, Yellowhead Pass was initially the favoured route. This image shows Chief Dominion Geologist Alfred Selwyn seated at centre, with artist and photographer John Hammond on his right and photographer Benjamin Baltzy on his left, together with five unidentified assistants, during a 1871 geological survey from the coast to Yellowhead Pass.

Fortunately, the railway crews fared better. One of the men charged with making a detailed survey through the mountains was Walter Moberly, brother of fur-trader and Hudson's Bay Company factor Henry John Moberly. Moberly's first task was to survey the proposed route over Howse Pass.[39] Although his superior (Fleming) preferred the gentler northerly route over Yellowhead Pass, Moberly was obsessed with the idea of running the railway through Howse Pass.[40] In the spring of 1872 Moberly was ordered to move his operation from Howse Pass to the Yellowhead Pass. He reluctantly obeyed, spending the entire season travelling to Yellowhead Pass and surveying east along the Athabasca River. By the spring of 1873, following a serious disagreement between Moberly and Fleming, the Yellowhead Pass survey was discontinued.[41]

Sandford Fleming was named chief surveyor in charge of finding the best route through the mountains for the proposed transcontinental railway. In 1872 he travelled across Canada to have a first-hand look at his favoured route, the gentle Yellowhead Pass. The group here, decked out in the travelling garb of the era is (l–r) Frank Fleming, Sandford Fleming, Dr. Grant and Dr. Arthur Moren.

Fleming nevertheless persisted in his preference for the northern route. For a brief period in 1880, it appeared he might have his way when surveyors located a line over Yellowhead Pass and along the Thompson River. But much to his dismay, the situation changed rapidly. When the Canadian Pacific Railway Company assumed the government's role in railway construction in 1880, neither Moberly's Howse Pass nor Fleming's Yellowhead Pass met the new company's criteria. By the end of the year both routes had been scrapped entirely. The railway was ultimately built over Kicking Horse Pass in 1884.

EAST–WEST TRAVEL

The Yellowhead Pass had thrice seen a large volume of traffic pass through in a short period of time: the fur traders between 1826 and 1830, the Overlanders in 1862 and the surveyors in 1872. In 1878, the pass saw a large volume of traffic of a different kind. For years, the Hudson's Bay Companys herd of horses had been multiplying on the rich pastures of Kamloops until they had become a nuisance. John Tait, the Kamloops factor, was put in charge of moving the large herd from the Kamloops post to Edmonton. He and his helpers

Altough Walter Moberly was one of Fleming's surveyors, he had his heart set on Howse Pass as a route for the railway. The men's difference of opinion led to a historic 1872 meeting between the two in Jasper. A local Métis created a Lobstick tree along the river in Jasper to commemorate the meeting, known locally as the Moberly Lobstick tree. Lobstick trees are created by trimming all the lower branches of a tree to create a landmark with which to honour someone. Although created in 1872, this Lobstick tree was still in good health more than 60 years later, as shown in this 1935 image. In 2004 the tree was still standing as a decaying snag.

rounded up 425 horses and began to drive them up what was becoming something of a pack trail along the Thompson River towards Tête Jaune Cache and the Yellowhead Pass. It is difficult to imagine what challenges would have confronted the men driving such a large group of animals along the narrow and treacherous trails around Moose Lake, down the Miette River and around Disaster Point on the Athabasca. Indeed, the herd that arrived at Fort Edmonton was nearly half the size of that which had left Kamloops several months earlier.[42]

Aside from continued use by Aboriginal peoples and a few prospectors, the silence of the Yellowhead Pass was seldom broken after the Canadian Pacific Railway's 1880 decision to locate its track further south. One notable exception occurred in the fall of 1880, when a band of homesteaders from New Westminster on the British Columbia coast decided to migrate east to take up farmland around Edmonton before the transcontinental railway brought a flood of settlers to the region.

Tom Henderson, his brother Bill and two like-minded young men set forth with nine horses, Tom's wife Margaret and six children ranging in age from 8 months to 13 years. Ada Law, Henderson's granddaughter provides details of the journey:

> From New Westminster to Yale, they travelled up the Fraser on a boat, and from Yale to Kamloops they used a wagon. The wagon was homemade and constructed of green wood which soon became so dry that it almost fell to pieces; the harness was made from the green hide of an ox with the hair still on the leather. The trip from Kamloops to Fort Edmonton was made by pack horse, leaving Kamloops in June 1880 and reaching Fort Edmonton that October. Grandma Henderson, with the baby Walter in her arms, rode a horse with Percy behind her. Olive and Robena were on another horse, with Charles, age three, and Annette, age five, standing in gunny sacks slung from the saddle horn. These sacks were stuffed with moss to cushion the children against bumps and bangs against trees. When the tots became tired standing, they could sit down in their sacks to rest. The entire group walked whenever possible.[43]

They followed the old surveyors' pack trail up the Thompson River – used only two years earlier by the 400 plus HBC horses – and proceeded over the pass to Jasper. Their sustenance came in the form of bannock and any supplies they could obtain from railway caches along the way.

The trip was difficult for Mrs. Henderson and the young children, but they endured 16 weeks on the trail to reach the mission at St. Albert on October 20. In the process, Margaret Henderson became the first non-Aboriginal woman to cross the Yellowhead Pass from west to east.[44]

The Henderson family (1884). Thomas and Percy (standing, back row) and Walter, Margaret (Peggy), Margaret, Charles, Olive, Janet and Agnes (front row, l-r), migrated from New Westminster, British Columbia to Edmonton, Alberta in 1880 to take up land before the railway arrived. Although the railway was re-routed to the south, the family nonetheless established a successful farming operation south of Edmonton.

Though they soon discovered that the CPR had been diverted to the south and there was little interest in the lands around Edmonton, the Hendersons' farming achievements eventually made their quarter-section south of Edmonton valuable in its own right. On their farm, Honey Glade at Rabbit Hill, they kept the first honey bees and Jersey cows in the district. Their 20-sided barn in which all the cows faced a central feeding station becaame a historical landmark which has since been moved to Fort Edmonton Park.[45]

This 1898 photo shows the innovative Henderson barn on the family's Rabbit Hill farm. Charles Henderson is on the left with his wife and baby Ella third from the left. The lady on the right is listed as Mrs. Henderson's mother, holding the hand of young Bill Sutherland. Second from the left is Mrs. Mike Ryan and child Stanley Ryan. The barn is now located at Fort Edmonton Park. (The lines are scratches on the old photo.)

The silence was also broken by a lone traveller who was to have a huge impact on the Jasper area. Lewis John Swift had spent some time at Lac St. Anne before venturing west with the Moberlys in 1890. Leaving them at their Jasper-area home, he continued over the pass to the Okanagan, only to reappear in Jasper in 1893, settling into the only building that remained of the old Jasper House.[46] Two years later he built a new home just east of the present town of Jasper. Beginning with a garden, he gradually built up a small farm with cattle and chickens. In 1897 he brought his Métis bride, Suzette Chalifoux, to the Jasper homestead.

In 1895, Lewis Swift brought his bride, Suzette Chalifoux, to the log house he had built in the Athabasca valley near present-day Jasper. They welcomed everyone who travelled through the valley and often treated them to freshly grown produce from the garden and milk and eggs from the farm. This image, taken in 1908, shows Suzette and four of her children near the family home, "Swift's Place."

Over the years, the Swift homestead became a landmark for travellers in the Athabasca valley. All were drawn to the only named place in the area, which assumed a significance similar to that of Old Bow Fort on the Bow River, except that the latter was simply the remains of an abandoned fort, whereas "Swift's Place" was a real living and vibrant family home, with four young children and a mother who produced home cooking and beautiful embroidery, among many other things.[47]

FLORA, FAUNA AND ROCKS

Visits from two scientists – biologist John Alden Loring and geologist James McEvoy – marked the end of the nineteenth century in the Athabasca and Miette River valleys. Loring arrived in August 1895 to undertake a two-year study of the natural history of the Jasper region.[48] He had hired a guide and crew in Edmonton: guides Daniel E. Noyes and his son, Daniel Jr.; cook "Texas Willie" Shanno; helper George Gagnon and two American prospectors, Walter Bisson and Samuel A. Dirr.

They left Edmonton on August 10 with supplies for two to three months. After crossing the Athabasca River, they proceeded to Jasper House, Henry House and the site of the present-day Jasper. Over the ensuing weeks, Loring travelled as far west as Yellowhead Pass and into the mountains along the Athabasca and Miette valleys, studying the birds and animals of the region. He returned the following year, again assisted by the Noyes family, and set up camp beside the Maligne River in late May. In late August, he headed north along the Snake Indian River (see Route IV below) and left the mountains by the Smoky River.

Two years later, Geological Survey of Canada geologist James McEvoy arrived.[49] He too hired packers in Edmonton: F.A. Jackson and Samuel Derr, and was accompanied by ornithologist William Spreadborough.[50] When McEvoy and his party arrived at the Athabasca River, they continued to the Miette and crossed Yellowhead Pass, where they found gold miners working. McEvoy investigated mines near the pass and towards Tête Jaune Cache while Spreadborough collected birds in the Yellowhead Pass area.

CLIMBING MOUNT ROBSON

In the early twentieth century, a major pack-train expedition was required to travel from the railway in Lake Louise to the Jasper area. Nevertheless, mountaineers and adventurers were beginning to take notice of the more northerly peaks. The Coleman Brothers had inadvertently forged a route from the eastern foothills to the junction of the Miette and Athabasca Rivers in 1893 when they missed the entrance to the Whirlpool River in their search for the legendary Mount Brown.[51] In 1906, the newly formed Alpine Club of Canada chose Mount Robson, Canada's highest known peak, as a fitting inaugural climb and club president A.O. Wheeler convinced the Coleman brothers to make the attempt.

On August 3, 1907 a party consisting of Arthur and Lucius Coleman and climber Reverend George Kinney set out from Lake Louise with rancher Jack Boker as packer. They took the Pipestone Pass route to the North Saskatchewan River, continued along the Sunwapta and Athabasca Rivers to the Miette, then built a small raft to ferry their supplies across the Athabasca River. There they encountered a group of three men who, with their 21 horses, were responsible for ferrying supplies through Yellowhead Pass to the surveyors working on the Grand Trunk Pacific Railway.[52] The Coleman party was grateful to learn all the details about the trail to Tête Jaune Cache, but dismayed the next morning to learn that in spite of their best efforts they had not managed to get out on the trail ahead of the surveyors' slow-moving pack train: 18 horses, each laden with 200 pounds of cargo! Fortunately, within a couple hours they had both caught up to and somehow managed to pass the other pack train on the narrow trail.

From then on, Coleman explained:

The trail was a joy in its picturesque variety. Sometimes it followed rocky ridges in the sun, where the mountain rims of the valley stood bare against the sky on each side, then it slipped down into the green twilight of spruces and balsams on the low ground or tunnelled through thickets of willow and alder, once in a while fording the Miette at some shallow place where it rustled mildly over a gravel bar. The water was so absolutely clear that every pebble could be seen on the bottom. Evidently no glacier fed its head waters.

After the vanishing trails of the past, it was an enormous comfort to follow a well-beaten road impossible to lose; and after days of hard chopping in slashes of fallen timber on the untraveled ways of the mountains it was a joyous relief to fasten up the axes and travel on a well-cut-out path that needed no adjustment. There were drawbacks, however, to the Yellowhead Trail. In the soft parts it was too well beaten down by hundreds of hoofs into pools of foul mud with the odour of a dunghill, and sometimes just to one side lay the festering carcass of a beast that had gone that way once too often.[53]

They soon crossed Yellowhead Pass, passed the shores of Yellowhead Lake and reached the Fraser River. "The trail," Coleman explained, "led down the Fraser Valley at the foot of Yellowhead Mountain, crossing boisterous creeks, fording Moose River, nearly up to the horses' backs, and running for a mile or two along a steep hillside above rich, marshy meadows where the river was building its delta at the head of Moose Lake."[54]

They continued on to the Grand Forks (Robson) River and made their way up the river to the rapids, where they continued on foot towards the lofty peak. Sadly, they were driven back by poor weather without having had the opportunity to make a serious attempt at climbing the peak. On September 16, they packed up and turned their weary horses towards home. Their supplies were nearly depleted by the time they reached the Athabasca River, but they knew they could restock at Swift's ranch:

Swift is a most interesting character, a white man of some energy and resource who married a woman of the country, an Iroquois half-breed [sic], many years ago, and had now a brood of wholesome-looking children playing about his log house. He had fenced and ploughed some fields, from which wheat and oats and barley had just been harvested, and had built a watermill on the stream that irrigated his farm to grind his wheat into flour, somewhat brown in colour, but making good bread; so that, except for sugar, tea, and tobacco, he was as nearly independent as a man can be...We had a long and interesting talk with Swift, admired the children, and the bread and potatoes from his garden, and praised deservedly the artistic buckskin suits embroidered with rich-coloured silks by Mrs. Swift – true works of art made from her own designs.[55]

After enjoying a brief respite from life on the trail, the Colemans set out for home via Edmonton, having decided that the snow would be too high on the passes to take their normal route through the mountains and foothills.

The Reverend George Kinney returned two years later (1909), fuelled by a burning desire to be the first person to climb Mount Robson. At John Moberly's place on the Athabasca, he had the good fortune to encounter a young guide by the name of Curly Phillips, who recorded that "Mr. Kinney was very anxious that I should go with him to Mount Robson; and so persistent was he that by the time I was ready to return to camp he had persuaded me to accompany him on the trip."[56]

They drove the horses across the river and got John Moberly to ferry them across in his dugout canoe. They spent the customary day at Swift's place – considered the end of civilization – before heading west into the mountains. After two days on some of the worst trail Phillips had ever experienced, they reached Yellowhead Pass. They proceeded to the Moose River, then followed the river north towards Mount Robson (see Route III below, pages 124–145).

One of the reasons Kinney was so anxious to climb Mount Robson that summer was that he had heard that a strong team of climbers was planning their own attempt. Indeed, on August 6, climbers L.S. Amery, G. Hastings and A.L. Mumm left the Lake O'Hara area to meet up with

Swiss Guide Moritz Inderbinen at Hector Station.[57] The foursome took the train to Calgary, then north to Edmonton. They made their way to the Athabasca River, where outfitter John Yates met them. All five continued west over Yellowhead Pass and, like Kinney before them, took the Moose River route to Mount Robson (see Route III below). They were not successful in climbing the mountain.

TÊTE JAUNE CACHE AND BEYOND

The same year the Coleman brothers made their lengthy journey from Lake Louise over the Yellowhead Pass to the Robson River, another epic adventure was in the making. Archie MacDonald had worked as a logger in his youth, prospected for silver and gold, herded cattle to remote Canadian Pacific Railway camps and built a ranch near Fort Colville, Washington before homesteading in Daysland, Alberta.

At age 68, MacDonald was determined to realize his dream of a ranch near a beautiful lake in the Cariboo. On April 27, 1907 the lame widower and his three sons, aged 17, 15 and 14, left on a hazardous pack-train trip across the Rockies via Yellowhead Pass.[58] At the McLeod River, west of Edmonton, they joined forces with experienced outfitter Fred Stephens, who was headed for the Smoky River country north of Mount Robson. Fortunately, by the time they reached the Athabasca and had to circumnavigate Disaster Point, they had the assistance of another traveller named Mac who had a large pack train with three helpers following and was headed for Tête Jaune Cache. He was carrying supplies for a man named Finch, who was going to build a store at the Cache to be ready for the survey crews when they arrived later that summer. Mac knew the best way to cross the Athabasca and had a canoe stashed nearby for just such a crossing.

The MacDonald-Stephens party left Mac at the Athabasca and proceeded to the Snake Indian River, which they also crossed, before continuing past the remains of Jasper House to the Snaring River. They gazed across to its far southern bank in astonishment. In MacDonald's words:

> Laid out there in the midst of the wilderness was a beautiful
> farm. Beside a large log house was a big vegetable garden and
> a wealth of hardy mountain flowers. There were fields of wheat
> and oats and hay, and twenty head of grade shorthorn cattle
> grazing in a pasture. The Durham bull that eyed us over the
> fence was a fine-looking animal. There were chickens scratching
> in the barnyard and a pen of pigs nearby.[59]

This, of course, was "Swift's Place" and the combined MacDonald-Stephens party camped nearby. Swift was waiting for Mac's pack train and the MacDonalds were able to give him information on its progress.

The MacDonalds bid adieu to Fred Stephens at Swift's Place. He continued travelling north, leaving them to face the next hurdle, the Miette River, alone. By proceeding upstream to a ford Swift had mentioned, they managed to cross without incident. They passed a small lake with a hand-printed sign reading Cowdung Lake. Before long they noticed that the stream they were following was flowing west. Without realizing it, they had crossed the pass and reached the Fraser River. They continued following the Fraser to arrive at Tête Jaune Cache on July 1, 1907. They then proceeded to the North Thompson River and eventually found their dream site on the Cariboo plateau, a short distance west of the North Thompson.

Another dream was fulfilled the following summer when Mary Schäffer and her companions Mollie Adams, Billy Warren and Sid Unwin completed their historic trek to Maligne Lake.[60] With plenty of summer still ahead of them, they attempted to proceed to the Jasper area by following the Maligne River to the north. When that route proved impassable, they retreated as far as Poboktan Creek. They followed the Poboktan to the Sunwapta, then made their way north to Jasper.[61] Having no easy means by which to cross the Athabasca River, they decided to head for Swift's Place, in hopes that he had a boat.

Proceeding east along the Athabasca, they detoured around the mouth of the fast-flowing Maligne River and soon spotted the Swift homestead on the Athabasca's far bank. They continued downriver to the Moberly homestead. They found only an empty home, a sign reading "Here's the crossing" posted to a tree by the river and a dugout canoe tied up on the other side. Two shots from a rifle soon brought Swift, who transported the people and goods across in three trips while the guides drove the horses across. Then, Schäffer explained:

> Our tents were barely up when a hospitable procession was seen making its way through the poplars. First came Mr. Swift carefully balancing a pitcher brimming with new milk, little Lottie followed with a pail of new potatoes all cleaned and ready for the pot, while tiny Ida brought up the rear with a basket containing a dozen fresh eggs. Later came Mrs. Swift carrying the youngest child, and, though her English was limited, we managed to get along nicely and returned the call in the afternoon. ... She had quantities of silk embroidery on the softest buckskin I have yet seen. Her silks she dyed herself, and her patterns were her own designing. ... Gloves, moccasins, and beautiful coats, we took everything and wished she had more; it was a grand afternoon's shopping for us all, for the lonely Athabaska woman and the two white women who had seen none of their kind for many a long day.[62]

Early in the twentieth century, Mary Schäffer, a Philadelphia Quaker who later moved to Banff, set two precedents in Rocky Mountain travel. Not only was she the first non-indigenous woman to explore extensively in the Rocky Mountains, but some considered her means of doing so – going into the wilderness for extended periods with a female companion and two unrelated men – to be scandalous. Today she is considered a pioneer and hero. She is seen here on her favourite horse, Nibs.

The following morning, the Schäffer party crossed paths with John Moberly and his family returning from a very successful hunt. After a brief hello, they proceeded toward the Miette River, where they realized that they had not yet known truly bad trails. Now, Schäffer explained, "The hills were steep and stony while the valley was exceedingly soft. The bones of many a worn-out servitor [horse] strewed the line of march and we wondered how it was to fare with our own before the set task was accomplished."[63]

They continued over the pass, around Yellowhead Lake and on to the Fraser. The trail around Moose Lake was as bad as they had been warned, but the continuation to Mount Robson was a great improvement. The following day they proceeded over another bad trail to the Cache. From the top of a small hill, they could look down "on the city of Tête Jaune Cache as she was in 1908. What we saw was a tiny log shack and a tent pitched beside it, both enclosed by a fence...a little beyond was another tent."[64]

They visited the lone inhabitant, Mr. Reading of Philadelphia, and Schäffer discovered that not only was he a friend of Swift's but they also had many mutual friends in Philadelphia. After having lunch with Mr. Reading, they met his friend, Mr. Finch. The following day, they again had lunch with Mr. Reading and were invited to a dinner party consisting of themselves and the remaining population of the town: two prospectors who were camped nearby. After a delicious meal, most of which had been packed on horses for hundreds of miles, a toast was drunk to a hoped for meeting in "civilized" lands.

The next day, they returned towards the Athabasca. They arrived on August 30 and made a brief stop at the site of Henry House before proceeding to Swift's hospitable homestead. As they crossed the Athabasca and headed for home, Schäffer lamented that the next time they came that way, "our horses would not have to swim for it, all would be made easy with trains and bridges; that the hideous march of progress, so awful to those who love the real wilderness, was sweeping rapidly over the land and would wipe out all trail troubles."[65]

But not before the Yellowhead Pass bore witness to another grand adventure. In the spring of 1909, guide Fred Stephens set out from Lacombe to accompany Sawyer, a mining engineeer who was to make a rough map of the route, Tom, a cook, Fred's brother Nick as packer, client Stanley Washburn and 22 horses.

They entered the mountains along the North Saskatchewan, travelled north to the Brazeau River and followed it to its headwaters at Nigel Pass. After crossing Nigel Pass, they proceeded north over Wilcox Pass and along the Athabasca, which they crossed upstream from Swift's homestead. After six days of camping near Swift's place, they packed up and returned to the trail with lightened packs and two fewer horses. They continued south along the Athabasca for about six miles (10 km), then turned sharply west along the Miette River. After several days of sometimes difficult travelling, they suddenly "realized that [the small brook they had been following] was running west instead of east. While travelling through what had seemed to us a level forest, we had crossed the backbone of the continent into British Columbia and at the very summit of the Yellowhead Pass."[66]

They left their horses at Yellowhead Lake to explore the valley of the Upper Fraser River on foot, then continued westward to the Moose River. They spent the night on its banks, forded the river and continued on a difficult trek along Moose Lake. After two rainy days camped at the west end of the lake, they were joined by a father and son who travelled with them for the next two weeks. Eventually, after 70 days on the trail, they reached Tête Jaune Cache. After several days exploring in the area, they returned to Swift's to replenish their supplies before contining over Roche Miette, out of the mountains and on to Edmonton.

As they travelled, Schäffer's prophetic lament was being fulfilled. The mountain climbers and adventurers crossing Yellowhead Pass in the summer of 1909 were not alone. While they explored the northern peaks and valleys, railway survey parties followed up on trial surveys from three

Above: Fred Stephens, who made his home base east of the mountains in Lacombe, Alberta, was one of the early Rocky Mountain outfitters. One of his repeat customers was Stanley Washburn, who had a burning desire to reach Tête Jaune Cache. After several attempts he finally fulfilled his dream. Stephens is seen here sitting on a makeshift backcountry table that he and his helpers likely built.

Opposite: Sir Arthur Conan Doyle, creator of Sherlock Holmes and one of the most popular writers of his time, was persuaded to visit Jasper in 1914. This image of a family picnic was taken on his second visit in 1923. Back row (l–r): unidentified, Arthur Conan Doyle (reclining), packers Ray Scott and Bob LeStrang and guide Closson Otto (with hat). In front are the three Conan Doyle children, Adrian, Jean and Dennis and their mother, Lady Jean Conan Doyle.

years earlier and picked out the railway's exact line as far west as the summit of Yellowhead Pass. The following year, a tote road was built along the right-of-way, filling the valley with railway workers all the way to the summit of Yellowhead Pass. In 1911 the Grand Trunk Pacific Railway was built through the Yellowhead Pass; the Canadian Northern Railway followed in 1913.

Once the Athabasca River Valley and the Jasper townsite were accessible by rail, the Canadian government was anxious to advertise the new park. Officials convinced well-known novelist Sir Arthur Conan Doyle and his wife Lady Jean to visit. There being no hotel available, the celebrated guests spent the week of June 11 to 19, 1914 lodged in a railway car in Jasper. The novelist also travelled by pack train along the Athabasca and Miette Rivers, over Yellowhead Pass, on to Tête Jaune Cache and back.[67]

Thirteen years later, the first cars reached the entrance to the mountains along the Athabasca; in 1931 something resembling a passable road from Edmonton to Jasper was opened. The first highway was built along the Yellowhead route in 1956 and twelve years later a new highway was built through the Miette River valley and over Yellowhead Pass, providing a direct route between Edmonton and the Pacific Coast.

In this image, the modern Yellowhead Highway (#16), which replaced the original 1931 road, can be seen crossing the Athabasca River, against the backdrop of the beautiful Athabasca River valley.

THE TRAIL TODAY

Fur trader David Thompson's campsite on the shore of Brûlé Lake, near the eastern entrance to today's Jasper National Park, became the original Jasper House. From there, trails on both sides of the river led to Old Fort Point, believed to be the location of Henry House (near today's town of Jasper). Today the Yellowhead Highway (Hwy. 16) follows the south and east banks of the Athabasca River as far as Cold Sulphur Spring, where the highway crosses the river.

From Cold Sulphur Spring to the Maligne River, a trail known as the Overlander Trail likely follows the route used by the Overlanders and others to attain Old Fort Point. This is the only section between Brûlé Lake and Tête Jaune Cache where some of the original trail still exists; most has been obliterated by rail lines and roads. The Overlander Trail holds two main interests for hikers: beautiful views of the Athabasca River valley and the John Moberly homestead. The original buildings still standing and remnants of old fences, cellars and foundations in the fields give an indication of the extent of the farm a century ago. From the Maligne River to Old Fort Point, the trail is largely a dirt track along the Athabasca River that passes roads, bridges and resorts: a very pleasant walk or cycle but not a wilderness hike in any sense.

The Canadian National Railway follows the Athabasca's north and west banks all the way to Jasper. Highway 16 shares this space from Cold Sulphur Spring to Jasper and the Celestine Lake Road runs from 9 kilometres north of the Jasper townsite's east exit to the Snake Indian River valley, following the river and the north shore of Jasper Lake. The road is a rough gravel road, suitable for most vehicles. It operates on a one-way system, with the direction changing on a prescribed schedule. Details are available at the Jasper Park Visitor Centre and are posted at the beginning of the one-way section. The Ewan Moberly Homestead historic site is located along this road (see Route IV, pages 170-171).

From Jasper to the Yellowhead Pass, Highway 16 follows the south bank of the Miette River most of the way, with the railroad on the north side. After the pass, the road and railroad are sometimes on the same side of the Fraser River and sometimes on opposite banks. Highway and railroad construction have obliterated the old horse trails for the entire distance. It takes a large dose of imagination to visualize what the trails were like prior to railroad construction in the early twentieth century.

Above: One of the delights of hiking the Overlander Trail along the Athabasca River is the remains of the John Moberly homestead. Artefacts such as the old fence shown here give an indication of both the extent of the homestead and the ways in which readily available materials were used in construction.

Below: The most obvious artefact on the John Moberly homestead is the remains of the family house. The building is small by today's standards. The outstanding feature is the skilled axe work shown in the squared logs and especially in the dovetailing for the corner joints. Such proficiency with an axe is uncommon today.

Trail Guide

Distances are adapted from existing trail guides: Patton and Robinson, Potter and Beers and from Gem-Trek maps. Distances intermediate from those given in the sources are estimated from topographical maps and from hiking times. All distances are in kilometres.

From Cold Sulphur Spring to Old Fort Point along the Athabasca River (The Overlander Trail)

Maps   83 D/16 Jasper

            83 E/1 Snaring

            Gem Trek Jasper and Maligne Lake

There is very little elevation change along this route.

Trailhead

The Cold Sulphur Springs trailhead is at a pull-out on the east side of Highway 16, 18.3 km north of the east exit to Jasper townsite. The south end of the trail can be accessed by following Highway 93A (Hazel Avenue) south from its intersection with Jasper's main street (Connaught Drive), crossing the CNR tracks and the Yellowhead Highway (Hwy. 16) to the Old Fort Point–Lac Beauvert Road junction. Turn left and follow this road 1.0 km to the Athabasca River bridge. Cross the bridge and turn right into the trailhead parking area. The trail starts at the information kiosk at the rear of the parking area.

0.0   Start heading west along the trail.

0.7   Begin climbing to the top of a steep ridge that offers a great view over the Athabasca River valley. There are a number of trails here. Head west by the big rock and stay high on the ridge. All trails seem to merge later on, and all are burdened by the constant roar of traffic from the highway.

3.2 Enter a forest (consisting largely of Douglas firs) that is open enough to give continuing good views out over the valley.

3.9 Opposite the Snaring River. Continue through the forest; pass a small stream bubbling out of the mountain side.

5.6 A burned out area with a viewpoint offering a good view of the Athabasca River below and the Jasper landing strip to the west.

8.2 Drop down to a flat meadow above the river; continue along the meadow amidst some shrubs and trees. Pass the remains of a very old log fence.

8.8 The remains of John Moberly's homestead: two old buildings and other artefacts. Enter near the end of the meadow. Enter the forest a short distance beyond the homestead.

11.9 The remains of an old fence and small cabins. Continue on level ground through a mixed forest with occasional very large Douglas fir trees.

13.7 The trail drops down and follows the edge of a braided stream, then the Athabasca River to the Maligne River. Turn left (southeast) and follow the Maligne River upstream.

15.5 Cross the Maligne River on a bridge to the Sixth Bridge Picnic Area. Continue west on trail #7, which follows the left (east) bank of the Athabasca River all the way to Old Fort Point. There are trail maps at various points along the way.

18.9 The trail crosses the Maligne Lake Road just after the road crosses the river, then continues along the river.

22.5 Opposite Jasper Park Lodge. The trail passes Lac Beauvert and crosses a bridge over an outlet stream. There are many trails in this area. Keep right, close to the river on an old road, until you come to a bridge across the river and a roadway.

23.7 Old Fort Point.

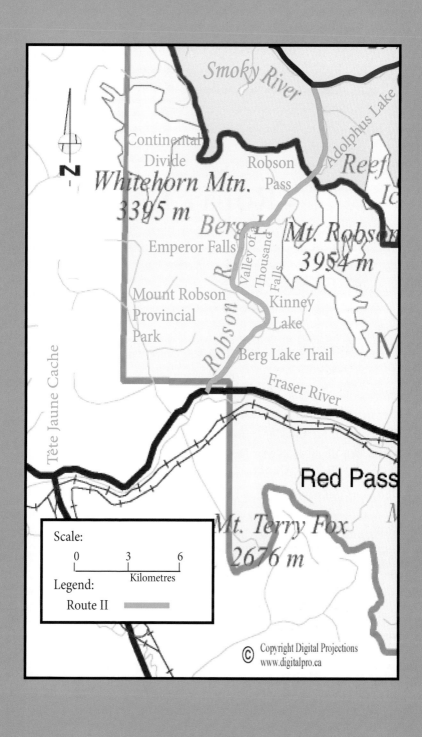

Smoky River

Adolphus Lake

Continental
Divide

Robson
Pass

Reef

Ic

Whitehorn Mtn.
3395 m

Berg L.

Mt. Robson
3954 m

Emperor Falls

Valley of a Thousand Falls

Mount Robson
Provincial
Park

Robson R.

Kinney
Lake

M

Berg Lake Trail

Tête Jaune Cache

Fraser River

Red Pass

Mt. Terry Fox
2676 m

M

Scale:

0   3   6

Kilometres

Legend:

Route II

ROUTE II

A Thousand Falls: Amery's Route from the Fraser River to the base of Mount Robson along the Robson River

I first hiked the North Boundary Trail with Janice and four of her teenaged friends in 1992. After scarcely seeing a soul on the trail for five days, it shocked our senses to arrive at Berg Lake and find people everywhere. The Berg Lake trail is reputed to be one of the busiest in the Canadian Rockies; the breathtaking scenery along the superbly maintained trail leaves little doubt as to why. Nevertheless, we opted not to camp among the hordes, but to push on towards the vehicle we had left at the trailhead. The group had stayed reasonably close together over the previous five days. Now, varying degrees of fatigue, foot pain and blisters caused the group to become separated; on the heavily used trail down the River, this was not a concern. I kept between the lead group of two and the remainder of the group.

As we approached the parking lot, I suddenly heard excited shouts that someone had broken into Anna's car. I quickened my pace and as I approached, asked what the problem was. A very distraught young woman responded that the trunk of her car had all kinds of "stuff" in it that had not been there when we left the car a week earlier. Sure enough, there was a pile of branches, moss, nuts, cones and grasses spread about in the trunk of her car. I asked if anything was missing and was told "No, nothing is missing but look at the mess."

Once everyone had calmed down and was able to look objectively at the situation, its true nature revealed itself. During the week we had been away, an industrious squirrel had somehow found a way into the trunk of the car and set about building a nest, complete with a stockpile of food for the coming winter. This busy animal had obviously been begging or stealing nuts from tourists and storing them away, as well as using natural materials to build its nest.

We cleaned out the debris from the trunk and checked the electrical functions of the car as thoroughly as we were able to, thinking that an electrical wire may have been chewed. We did not find any problems and were soon on our way, travelling cautiously at first, until we were comfortable that all systems were working properly. The car remained in Anna's family for many years, and no problems ever appeared, nor did the access route to the trunk ever become evident. As for the squirrel, one can only hope it had adequate time to rebuild its nest and stockpile of food before winter set in.

In the 1990s, the authors and Janice's friends hiked many of the trails that the *Life of the Trail* series explores. This image (l–r, back row Mike, Anna, Janice, Ryan and Catherine with Emerson kneeling in front) was taken after the group completed the North Boundary Trail and reached the Continental Divide.

CHRONOLOGY

1898   James McEvoy of the Geological Survey of Canada estimates the height of Mount Robson as 13,700 feet (4176 metres; its actual height is 12,972 feet or 3954 metres).

1907   The Coleman brothers accompany Reverend George Kinney in his attempt to travel up the Robson River on horseback to the base of Mount Robson. They begin chopping a trail through logs that were two or more feet in diameter. Thwarted, they continue the attempt on foot – again unsuccessfully.

1909   Mountaineer Leopold S. Amery is the first person to travel from Berg Lake to Kinney Lake along the Robson River.

1911   A combined group from the Alpine Club of Canada (ACC) and the Smithsonian Institute reach Kinney Lake after five difficult days following the Robson River from Berg Lake through the Valley of a Thousand Falls.

1913   Arthur Wheeler engages Curly Phillips to build a trail up the Robson River and through the Valley of a Thousand Falls to Berg Lake. Phillips and Frank Doucette build a series of switchbacks and a spectacular flying trestle bridge to provide the first real trail between Kinney Lake and Berg Lake.

Sixty-nine active members of the ACC walk along the newly constructed trail and enjoy two weeks at the Berg Lake camp. Among them is Caroline Hinman, who is introduced to both mountain climbing and touring by pack train on her first trip to the Canadian Rockies.

1914   J.W. Beatty and famed Group of Seven artist A.Y. Jackson are commissioned by the Canadian Northern Railway to paint in the construction camps along the as-yet uncompleted rail line. On one of his trips, Jackson hikes up the Robson River to Berg Lake.

1915   Caroline Hinman and Mary Jobe set out on a major trip into the wilds north of Mount Robson, outfitted by Curly Phillips.

1917   Mary Jobe accompanies Curly Phillips and Jack Hargreaves as they pack supplies to the Wapiti River for the Smithsonian Institute.

Artist William Johnstone hikes to Berg Lake accompanied by mountaineer H.S. Bulyea. They pass Kinney Lake to spend the night at the north end of Berg Lake.

1924   Famed Canadian climbers Phil and Don Munday attend the Mount Robson ACC camp and climb Mount Robson with Swiss Guide Conrad Kain.

1925   Caroline Hinman returns to the Kinney Lake–Berg Lake trail with one of her Off the Beaten Track tours. Her frequent companion, Lillian Gest, joins them.

1927   Roy Hargreaves builds the Berg Lake Chalet.

1930   The trail between Kinney Lake and Berg Lake is no longer a wilderness trail. From Robson Station, a broad trail – almost a road – leads to a well-engineered bridge across the Fraser River. Permanent camps adorn the summit of Robson Pass; hikers simply shoulder packs and carry their provisions to the camps.

HISTORY

Travellers setting out over Yellowhead Pass, around the north shore of Moose Lake and on down the Fraser River might expect the towering giant Mount Robson to dominate the landscape. But they are bound to be disappointed. Mile after mile pass without even a glimpse of the mountain. Then, just as navigational doubts begin to rear their ugly heads, the massive peak suddenly bursts into view, or as Arthur Coleman put it, "at last Mount Robson burst upon us in reality, and we knew that the monarch deserved his reputation."[1]

The quantity of snow and ice decorating Mount Robson – and the cloud that frequently adorns its peak – hint at its immensity. Unfortunately the high peak traps clouds that often bring rain and mist to the area.

Mount Robson is set back some distance from the Fraser River; though early travellers and fur traders saw the mountain, there is no record of anyone actually visiting it, and in spite of historians' best efforts, the source of its name remains obscure. According to historian Frank W. Anderson:

> Henry John Moberly, HBC trader, thought it might have been named for a trapper named Robson who had run a trapline near the base of the mountain. But when J.G. MacGregor researched one of his many books, *Overland by the Yellowhead*, he discovered no evidence of such a trapper. One theory this well known historian advanced is that the mountain is named after Colin Robertson who established St. Mary's House for the Hudson's Bay Company on the Peace River at the mouth of the Smoky in 1819. Afterwards he sent some of his men up the Smoky with instructions to cross into New Caledonia, as British Columbia was then known, to establish trade with the Indians living along the Upper Fraser River. It is possible that these men, when seeing the mighty mountain at the headwaters of the Smoky, named it for the chief trader. The name Robertson could easily have become shortened to Robson, especially when translated from Iroquois to English.[2]

FIRST ATTEMPTS TO REACH MOUNT ROBSON

Early twentieth century mountaineers were far more concerned with the peak's height than who it was named for. In 1898 James McEvoy of the Geological Survey of Canada estimated its height at 13,700 feet (4176 metres) a close approximation of its actual height of 12,972 feet (3954 metres). At the inaugural meeting of the Alpine Club of Canada, President Arthur O. Wheeler suggested that climbing Mount Robson would be a fitting way to launch the new club. It took little convincing for brothers Arthur and Lucius Coleman to embrace the task. Accompanied by climber Reverend George Kinney and packer Jack Boker, they set out from Laggan Station (Lake Louise) on August 3, 1907 with a pack train of ten horses. Forty-one days later, they arrived at the mouth of the Grand Forks (Robson) River.[3] They were behind schedule and running short of supplies. Expedience was of the utmost necessity.

The most obvious route to the base of the mountain appeared to be up the Robson River. They began chopping a trail through fallen burnt British Columbia timber, often two feet or more in diameter. Though they found an old trail that had been made many years earlier by an unknown party, it was too full of windfalls to use. Once they reached green timber, the situation changed enough that they were able to pick "up the old trail, which wound between big cedars and hemlocks, hoary with long, grey lichens hanging from their limbs, and deeply padded with soft green moss under foot, except where thickets of ferns and devil's clubs hid the fallen logs in the wetter places."[4]

By September 10, they had forced their tired horses up the trail "where logs had to be jumped and rocks scrambled over,"[5] to a spot where they set up camp near rapids on the river. From there they proceeded on foot, carrying five days' worth of supplies loaded into 40-pound (18 kilogram) packs. They soon reached the shore of a beautiful lake

> ...which had been visited by Mr. Kinney the day before, and has been named Lake Kinney in honour of our indefatigable comrade... We advanced up the valley, picking our way among the vast blocks which had rolled down from the cliffs of Mount Robson, finding very bad going until we drew near to the greatest waterfalls of all, where the main river plunged down from the north-east through rugged canyons, with a drop of two thousand feet. Looking up at the final wall of rock that ended the valley, one could see the white gleam of four or five of these falls, but the rest of the river was hidden except for spray rising here and there like mist.[6]

Kinney Lake is situated in a narrow valley, surrounded by mountains. Its north end (from which this shot was taken) is dominated by the extensive gravel flats of the Robson River. The lake takes its name from the first man to record visiting the lake, and reminds thousands of tourists each year of the monumental effort that Kinney made to climb Mount Robson.

Spectacular scenery they had found in abundance; an approach to Mount Robson would take renewed effort. The trio retreated to their campsite near the rapids and decided to try a gentler slope up a smaller branch of the Robson River. As they set out the following morning, clouds rolled in, spelling an end to the fine weather they had been enjoying. More than a foot of snow fell that night. With no clearing in sight and provisions for only three days remaining, they were forced to admit defeat. They returned to their main camp on the Robson River and on September 16 headed for home.

Reverend George Rex Boyer Kinney (1872–1961)

George Kinney was born at Victoria Corner, New Brunswick on October 14, 1872, the second of nine children born to the Reverend Aaron and Elizabeth Kinney. As was often the case with ministers, Kinney's father moved frequently. Young Kinney spent his first five years on Grand Manan Island, NB then another five in Moncton, NB before heading to Nova Scotia. His father's postings in that province included Halifax, Port Maitland, Baddeck and Shubenacadie.

At age 23, Kinney enrolled in the Methodist Asbury College in Willmore, Kentucky. He graduated three years later with a Bachelor of Arts in Theology and in 1899 was accepted into the British Columbia Conference of the Methodist ministry on a trial basis. Over the next six years he pastored to several small British Columbia communities. In 1905 he was ordained at Columbia College, New Westminster. His first charge after ordination was at Michel, BC in the Crowsnest Pass, but there is no reliable record of his brief postings at small BC communities over the next several years.

While serving in temporary positions in Banff and Field in 1904, he investigated the fossil beds on Mount Stephen. In October he achieved the monumental feat of executing the first solo ascent of that mountain. For Kinney, it was the first of what was to become a record of nearly impossible climbs.

Kinney was one of the original members of the Alpine Club of Canada (ACC), though he did not attend the founding meeting in Winnipeg in March 1906. He did attend the first ACC mountaineering camp in Yoho that summer and helped guide new recruits to the top of The Vice President. He also

Reverend George Kinney was a man of God who preferred to work with underprivileged people in small isolated communities. As a young man, he became obsessed with being the first person to climb Mount Robson. His efforts on that mountain are still regarded as one of the outstanding achievements of Canadian mountaineering history.

lent his assistance at the 1907 camp in Paradise Valley; the membership list for that year credits Kinney with several climbs around Crowsnest Pass and Lake Louise.

While Kinney was working at James Bay in Victoria, BC in 1907, Arthur Wheeler, the president of the ACC, asked him to join Arthur Coleman and his brother Lucius in an attempt on Mount Robson. As they searched for a route to the base of the mountain along the Robson River, Kinney was the first to spot the lake which the Colemans named Kinney Lake; he himself named the Valley of a Thousand Falls.

The trio was unsuccessful in climbing the mountain either that year or the next. Though they had scheduled a renewed attempt for 1909, Kinney, who had become obsessed with the idea of being first to ascend the peak, decided to head out alone. Concerned that a team of foreign climbers who were headed for Mount Robson would reach it – and perhaps climb it – before the Colemans arrived from the east, he flagrantly breached climbing etiquette and abandoned his commitment to the Colemans.

He met up with a young man, Curly Phillips, who did not even have an ice axe, let alone any mountaineering experience. Nonetheless, in what has been described as one of the most outstanding achievements in the history of mountaineering in the Canadian Rockies, they apparently succeeded in reaching the summit after several attempts. Kinney's unwavering claims that they had reached the peak continue to be disputed, but whatever they accomplished was an exceptional feat of mountaineering.[7] Although he acted as an assistant guide at the 1910 ACC climbing camp in the Consolation Valley, Kinney subsequently faded from the climbing scene and is not mentioned at any future climbing camps.

More redeeming aspects of his personality shone through in other ways. In 1910, a school-girl in Keremeos suffered severe burns and required a skin graft. Kinney not only volunteered to donate the required cuticle, but also sat on a table next to the little girl, comforting her while the doctor removed 24 square inches (154 square centimetres) of skin from his leg without anaesthetic.

Despite his conscientious objector status during the First World War, Kinney served as a stretcher bearer in the 4th Field Ambulance Corp. During his off-duty hours, he toured the front lines giving talks on the Canadian Rockies. While in London on leave, he lectured to the Royal Geographical Society and was made a fellow of the Society.

In 1920 48-year-old Kinney married Alice Loree, secretary of the Vancouver Normal School. They had three children: Bliss, Betty and Don. Throughout their childhood, he continued his ministry, which for many years took him to isolated logging camps and fishing villages along the coast of Vancouver Island. During the Depression, he worked with men on relief. The family struggled financially, but kept a large garden wherever they lived and worked it diligently.

After his marriage, Kinney was pastor of Grace Methodist Church in Cumberland on Vancouver Island. Sometime during the period 1920-23 he joined a party led by Harold Banks to make the first ascent of the Comox Glacier. In the early thirties he was transferred to Proctor, BC where he developed the Kootenay Waterways mission. From 1937 to 1942 he worked with the Koksilah Indian Mission in Duncan.

Kinney retired from active church work at the age of 70, although he continued to serve as a replacement preacher. He died in Victoria on November 14, 1961 at age 89. He was a man of God who never pushed religion down anyone's throat but gently slipped it into conversations. His love of the outdoors, which he referred to as God's Cathedral, lent itself well to the role of backwoods preacher and although he gave up mountaineering quite early in life, he never forgot his Mount Robson days and always kept an ice axe and a pair of climbing boots hanging in his house. The thousands of hikers and mountain climbers who pass by Kinney Lake on the beautiful Berg Lake trail leading to the base of Mount Robson each year are reminded of the amazing climbing feat of this devoted preacher.

The 1907 ACC expedition was the first recorded attempt to reach the base of Mount Robson by following the Robson River. Future groups preferred the Moose River route (see Route III below), which was longer but provided a reasonably good trail upon which horses could travel to Berg Lake at the base of the mountain. A member of one such group, mountaineer L.S. Amery, became one of the first people to travel from Berg Lake to Kinney Lake along the Robson River. He and his companion Keller completed the trek on foot in 1909.[8]

A SCIENTIFIC EXPEDITION

A much larger party repeated Amery's trip in 1911. The prestigious party was made up of A.O. Wheeler, president of the ACC; Byron Harmon, the ACC photographer; Conrad Kain, the ACC official climbing guide; George Kinney as assistant and scientists Ned Hollister, J.H. Riley, Charles Walcott Jr. and Harry Blagden from the Smithsonian.[9] They engaged Curly Phillips as the main outfitter. Because 30 horses were needed to carry the men and their baggage, Phillips brought outfitters James Shand-Harvey and Fred Stephens to assist. They used the Moose Pass route to access Berg Lake, then continued to the top of the steep cliffs leading to the Valley of a Thousand Falls. From there, the outfitters and horses returned over Moose Pass while the men continued along the Robson River on foot. Five days of difficult travel through the Valley of a Thousand Falls led them to Kinney Lake, where their horses awaited them.

This 1909 British party consisting of (l-r, back row) climbers A.L. Mumm and L.S. Amery with Swiss guide Moritz Inderbinen, outfitter John Yates, two unidentified packers, [sitting, (l–r)] another unidentified packer, climber Geoffrey Hastings, packer James Shand-Harvey and a fourth unidentified packer was heading towards Mount Robson intent on climbing the mountain when George Kinney informed them that he had already done so.

Above: In 1911 Alpine Club of Canada (ACC) president Arthur Wheeler organized an expedition of Smithsonian scientists and ACC members to explore the Mount Robson area. Part of Wheeler's objective was to determine if an ACC camp could be held in the area. The portion of the group shown here consists of (l–r): President Wheeler, outfitter Curly Phillips, scientists Harry Blagden, J.H. Riley, and Charles Walcott, Jr., with packers James Shand-Harvey and Casey Jones standing and ACC helper Reverend George Kinney seated.

Opposite: The Moose Pass route was too long and difficult to provide adequate access to the Alpine Club of Canada climbing camp at Mount Robson. Curly Phillips was given the task of building an alternate trail up the Robson River. The flying trestle bridge seen here under construction in 1913 was part of this new trail. The bridge lasted well into the twentieth century, but was eventually replaced with a series of switchbacks on a re-routed trail.

THE ALPINE CLUB OF CANADA CAMPS

One of the excursion's objectives was to determine whether the Berg Lake area might be a suitable location for the ACC's annual camp. The reconnaissance proved favourable; the flats between Berg Lake and Robson Pass were selected as the site for the 1913 camp. The group was concerned, however, that the trail up the Moose River was far too long for this type of activity. So Wheeler hired Curly Phillips, the Jasper guide who had attempted Mount Robson with Rev. Kinney in 1909 and who kept a winter trapline in the area, to build a trail up the Robson River and through the Valley of a Thousand Falls to Berg Lake. With the help of Frank Doucette, Phillips built a series of switchbacks and a spectacular flying trestle bridge around the rock face leading to Emperor Falls. This effort provided the first real trail between Kinney Lake and Berg Lake and is the basis of today's trail.

The 69 active members of the ACC who walked along the newly constructed trail in the summer of 1913 greatly appreciated Phillips' effort. They enjoyed two weeks at the camp, from July 28 to August 9, during which time: "From Mount Robson siding they wandered in happy groups to Kinney Lake and up the cliffs to Berg Lake. It was a fifteen-mile walk along a track Curly Phillips had made...but in the splendour of the alpine surroundings, weariness vanished. And at last the reward. In the words of an earlier visitor: 'Cold, icy, clean-cut...Mount Robson, a noble, massive vision to the pilgrims who had come so far to seek her'."[10]

The ACC camp returned to the base of Mount Robson in 1924, paving the way for a historic event. Famed Canadian climbers Phil and

Don Munday had travelled to the Mount Robson area by train in February 1920. Unable to arrange for pack horses, they shouldered their 30 kg packs and hiked up Phillips' trail to Berg Lake, where they set up camp and did some climbing.[11]

More than 100 people often attended early Alpine Club of Canada camps, a group size that required a large flat space to set up the tents. The gravel flats between Berg Lake and Robson Pass provided ample space for such a large camp. Berg Glacier, which flows down the side of Mount Robson and gives Berg Lake its name, is shown on the left of the image.

They were so fascinated with the area that they joined the 1924 ACC camp. At that time, the couple and Swiss guide Conrad Kain ascended Mount Robson. As Don recounts: "The weather was perfect, the climb uneventful. Phyl on the first rope, followed in Conrad's steps. As he reached the summit he turned, and gallantly held out his hand to Phyl: 'There lady,' he exclaimed, 'You are the first woman on top of Mount Robson!' Phyl's only words were; 'Thank Heaven!' For her, this was the culmination of a four year ambition."[12]

The husband and wife team of Don and Phyl Munday, seen here on the top of Mount Victoria, near Lake Louise, were accomplished climbers who climbed mainly on the west coast of British Columbia. Phyl had her heart set on climbing Mount Robson; her dream came true at the Alpine Club of Canada's 1924 camp, making her the first woman to summit the peak.

A notable participant of the 1913 ACC camp was Caroline Hinman, who was to lead her famous Off the Beaten Track tours over virtually every known trail in the Canadian Rockies. This first trip to the Canadian Rockies served as her introduction to both mountain climbing and touring by pack train. She climbed with Swiss guides, and Curly Phillips took her and others on a five-day trail ride over passes and glaciers north of Mount Robson. The camp experience changed her life forever: "So deep an impression did that experience make upon me, so much benefit did I derive therefrom, physically, mentally and spiritually, that before the following winter had half begun, I had determined to go back and to take with me others who, without being led, might never find the way to that health-bringing wonderland of unpolluted air, warm sunshine and brilliant flowers."[13]

BEYOND MOUNT ROBSON

The 1913 camp also introduced Hinman to Mary Jobe, another alpine explorer who would return to the Mount Robson area on several occasions. Only once, however, did they travel together; on July 1, 1915 the two women set out on a major trip into the wilds north of Mount Robson. They were outfitted by Curly Phillips with assistance from Frank Doucette, Joe Soper and Arnold, David and John Tyler, three young helpers from New York who had come at Hinman's request. Their eight saddle horses and 15 pack horses constituted a significant sized pack train.[14]

This 1915 image shows Caroline Hinman on the left with Mary Jobe and outfitter Curly Phillips. The three met at the 1913 Alpine Club of Canada camp and completed a major pack-train trip in 1915. A romance developed between Phillips and Jobe, who travelled together several times.

The large party followed the now familiar trail up the Robson River, past Kinney Lake, over the trestle bridge to Emperor Falls and on to Berg Lake. The following day, Phillips and Hinman toured Berg Lake on a raft Phillips had built. The real trip began on July 3, when the horses were loaded with over 2000 pounds (907 kg) of supplies and equipment. Phillips believed in feeding everyone well:

The staples of the regular trail diet included flour, cornmeal, rolled oats, sugar, beans, rice, macaroni, potatoes and bacon. Dried fruits – currants, raisins, peaches, apricots, apples, prunes – and almonds were plentiful. Coffee, tea, cocoa and cans of evaporated milk jostled against all kinds of spices and flavourings. There were tins of jam, vegetables, fruit, corned beef, ham, Klim, butter and soups; and delicacies such as pickles, jelly powders, coconut, maple syrup, custard powder, cheeses and jars of olives. For the laundry there were nine bars of yellow soap and for the women three bars of Palmolive each. There were candles to light the cook tent so they could do their chores after supper or read and write up their diaries. It was small wonder that the comforts of Curly's camps were famous in the world of backwoods travel.[15]

North of Robson Pass they turned west and crossed Bess Pass and Jack Pine Pass to the base of Mount Kitchi (Mount Sir Alexander), which Jobe and Phillips had attempted to climb in 1914.

Though they met no more success climbing Mount Kitchi in 1915, all enjoyed the trip. By August 19, they had returned to the Smoky River, arriving back at Robson Station on September 1. According to biographer Cindy Smith:

It was a relaxed group and everyone got along well. There were many layover days in camp. There were the routine chores to be done, such as washing, sewing and oiling of boots. There was time for writing up a diary or going hiking, climbing, hunting or fishing...The evenings were spent around a campfire in the forest glade or inside one of the tents if it was raining. Card games were popular...Robert Service's poems and Dickens's Pickwick papers were popular...Many hours were spent singing songs or simply talking. Caroline's diary is filled with the evident joy of being in the woods, a feeling of great personal well-being, away from the troubles of the outside world.[16]

This image of Mount Robson (looking southeast) clearly shows the amount of snow and ice on the northern flank of the mountain, with Berg Glacier flowing into Berg Lake. Ice floes can be seen in the lake at almost any time during the summer.

At the time "It was certainly unusual, if not downright scandalous, for two attractive young women to set off on a two-month adventure with six men unrelated to them."[17] Unusual, but not without precedent. On the east coast, Mina Hubbard crossed Labrador in 1905 with four men hired for the trip, and Mary Schäffer and Mollie Adams had been travelling in the Rockies with Billy Warren and Sid Unwin in the early twentieth century (see above, pages 71-75). In all three cases, a romance developed between a woman and a guide: Mina Hubbard and George Elson, Mary Schäffer and Billy Warren and now Mary Jobe and Curly Phillips.

Their courtship, which became obvious over the course of the expedition, lasted another three years. Their many travels during this time included a repeat of the 1915 excursion in the late fall of 1917, when Mary Jobe accompanied Curly Phillips and Jack Hargreaves as they packed supplies to the Wapiti River for the Smithsonian Institute. Immersed in splendid fall colours, they accomplished their task and continued down the Smoky River, leaving the mountains at Grand Cache.

Mary Lenore Jobe Akeley (1878–1966)

Mary Jobe was born on January 29, 1878 on the family farm of Richard Jobe and Sara Jane Pittis near Tappan, Ohio. Young Mary enjoyed rural life, walking three miles (5 km) each day to school, where she excelled academically and was a strong athlete. She graduated from Scio College (now Mount Union College) in Alliance, Ohio in 1897 and went on to do graduate work at Bryn Mawr College between 1901 and 1903, while simultaneously teaching night classes at nearby Temple University. She taught history at a state college in Cortland, New York for the next three years, then taught at Hunter College in New York, N.Y. until 1916. During this time she earned a Masters Degree in English and history from Columbia University and began working towards a doctorate (which she did not complete).

Jobe spent most summers during this period in the Canadian

Rockies and Selkirks. In 1905 she sstayed in the Selkirks for three months and travelled through the Rockies on her way home. She returned in 1909 and joined a group – including soon-to-be well-known mountaineer Bess MacCarthy – intent on climbing Mount Sir Sandford in the Selkirks. The two women spent several weeks in the Columbia Valley before heading to the Alpine Club of Canada (ACC) camp at Lake O'Hara, where Jobe climbed Mount Schäffer and took a two-day circle trip over five high passes. The following summer (1910) she was on pack-train trips in the vicinity of Mount Assiniboine and Baker Lake and in 1912 between Lake Louise and Jasper. In the winter, Jobe presented lectures and lantern-slide shows about her travels in New York schools, resorts and institutions and wrote magazine articles exhorting readers to visit the mountains themselves.

The summer of 1913 marked a turning point in Jobe's travels. She journeyed to northern British Columbia and Alaska to gather information on local Aboriginal peoples. Her explorations led her to Tête Jaune Cache and to join the ACC annual camp at Robson Pass. There she heard stories of a magnificent peak far to the north – and met outfitter Curly Phillips, who had seen the mountain firsthand. She hired Phillips for the following summer and together with Winnipeg climber Margaret Springate set out to locate the mountain and perhaps achieve a first ascent. They accomplished the first goal but were unsuccessful in climbing the mountain, which Jobe named Mount Kitchi, taken from a Cree word meaning mighty.

Undeterred, Jobe returned in the summer of 1915 with Phillips and another companion from the 1913 ACC camp, traveller and explorer Caroline Hinman. The party was again

Curly Phillips and Mary Jobe with Phillips' dog,
likely taken on their 1915 trip north of Mount
Robson. Jobe's fall 1917 trip with Phillips was her
final visit to the Canadian Rockies.

unsuccessful in achieving its climbing objective, but perhaps Phillips and Jobe were distracted by another path – that of a trail romance.

The following winter marked Jobe's final year of teaching before launching Camp Mystic, a summer camp for girls aged 8 to 18 in Mystic, Connecticut. The camp flourished until 1930 but kept Jobe too busy to travel to the Rockies in the summer. She returned to Jasper in the fall of 1917 to accompany Curly Phillips and Jack Hargreaves on a late fall trip to cache supplies at a wilderness destination far north of Mount Robson, but never again set foot in the Canadian Rockies. It is speculated that this trip signalled the end of her romance with Curly Phillips and that the end of the relationship weighed in her decision not to return.

It was about this time that Jobe met Carl Akeley, an employee of the American Museum of Natural History in New York and an African specialist who was actively involved in exploring and collecting animal and bird specimens on that continent for the museum. His adventures in exotic places appealed to Jobe; she became enamoured with the man and his work. The fact that she was 46 years old and 14 years his junior proved no obstacle; they were married on October 18, 1924. Two years later, Jobe joined her husband on his fifth expedition to Africa. Sadly, he contracted a lethal tropical disease and died a mere 25 months after their marriage. Jobe buried her husband in the Belgian Congo and remained to complete the work of his expedition.

Back in the United States, Jobe continued to immerse herself in her husband's work, becoming a vocal crusader for the establishment of game preserves in Africa. She studied and wrote about the people of Africa and made several trips to the continent between 1926 and 1951. She gave frequent radio lectures and interviews and lectured widely to all types of organizations throughout the eastern United States. Her only return to Canada took place in 1937 when she re-lived a canoeing trip to the Big Bend on the Columbia River she had enjoyed with Beth MacCarthy and others back in 1909.

During this time, Jobe was a member of alpine clubs in Canada, the United States and France, the American Game Protective Association and American Society of Mammalogists and other learned societies. Mount Union College awarded her an honorary Doctor of Literature degree in 1930 and King Albert of Belgium made her a Knight of the Order of the Crown for her work in Africa.

Perhaps her most enduring recognition, however, is Mount Jobe in the Rockies. In 1923, members of the Alberta–British Columbia Boundary Commission named this peak southeast of Mount Sir Alexander (Mount Kitchi), in her honour, commemorating the woman who had done so much to add to the knowledge of this part of the Canadian West. She died at a nursing home in Mystic, Connecticut on July 19, 1966 at age 88.[18]

As for Caroline Hinman, she returned to the Kinney Lake–Berg Lake trail in 1925 with one of her Off the Beaten Track tours. This time she was accompanied by her frequent companion Lillian Gest. The group stayed in cabins near Adolphus Lake, from which they toured Moose Pass.[19] Outfitting the group were the four Hargreaves brothers, who had established a ranch near the base of Mount Robson in 1921 and frequently guided parties to the CNR cabins at Berg Lake. In 1927, Roy Hargreaves built the Berg Lake Chalet which was used by commercial horse parties until the 1970s. The heritage cabin has been restored by British Columbia Provincial Parks as a day use facility, renamed the Hargreaves Shelter.

Caroline Hinman, who became famous for escorting American teenaged girls through the mountains on her Off the Beaten Track tours, spent many summers touring in the Canadian Rockies.

PAINTING THE MAGNIFICENT

Once Curly Phillips opened the trail from Kinney Lake to Berg Lake in July 1913, artists inevitably wanted to visit and paint this beautiful area. Spurring them on was the Canadian Northern Railway, which commissioned artists to paint scenes along the line through the Yellowhead Pass for use in advertising and in decorating passenger cars. In 1914, J.W. Beatty obtained a commission for himself and famed Group of Seven artist A.Y. Jackson to paint in the construction camps along the as-yet incomplete rail line. Beatty was satisfied to stick close to the rail line, but Jackson wandered farther afield:

> Working from the tracks was not very exciting, so I took to climbing the mountains. The chief engineer did not approve of my going alone, and he arranged that I should always be accompanied by one of the staff. There was no lack of volunteers. The young engineers were tough, husky boys who had much to teach me. I learned from them how to get about in the mountains with neither blankets nor tent, on a diet restricted to bread, oatmeal, bacon and tea. Most of my trips were made with Bert Wilson, one of the engineers.[20]

On one such trip, they hiked up the Robson River to Berg Lake, painting and sketching as they went.[21]

Berg Lake was visited by another artist, William Johnstone, in 1917. Unable to obtain horses, he and mountaineer H.S. Bulyea took only enough food for one day.[22] They hiked past Kinney Lake to spend the night at the north end of Berg Lake, then returned by the same route the following day.

By the end of the 1920s, the path between Kinney and Berg lakes was no longer a wilderness trail. J. Monroe Thorington reported that from Robson Station a broad trail – almost a road – led to a well-engineered bridge across the Fraser.[23] Permanent camps on the summit of Robson Pass meant that pack horses were no longer required; hikers simply shouldered packs and carried their provisions to the camps.

The Trail Today

Today a service centre is located near where the Robson River flows into the Fraser, complete with campgrounds, information centre, gas station and restaurant – all in full view of the majestic mountain.

The Berg Lake trail is one of the best maintained, busiest and most beautiful trails in the Canadian Rockies. The first part of the trail follows the rushing Robson River as it makes its turbulent way to the Fraser. The trail is an old road that gently climbs towards Kinney Lake. This part of the trip is worth doing on its own. The lake is beautifully situated with a picnic ground at the south end. For those day-hikers who have the time, a worthwhile extension of the hike is to continue along the shore of Kinney Lake, over a steep headland to the end of the lake, and along the gravel flats at the head of the lake. This bowl-like amphitheatre has a charm of its own and provides a good view down the Robson River valley.

The end of the gravel flats marks the end of the day hike for most people. Backpackers or strong day-hikers begin the steep and unrelenting climb through the very beautiful Valley of the Thousand Falls to the gravel flats at the end of Berg Lake. The scenic beauty of the trail, dotted by viewpoints, is unparalleled. Unfortunately, the famous Phillips flying trestle bridge has been replaced with switchbacks on a re-routed trail.

After reaching Berg Lake, views are dominated by the lake, with glaciers descending right to water level, and of course, the magnificent Mount Robson. Between the south end of Berg Lake and Robson Pass are several campgrounds and the Hargreaves Shelter. Several pleasant day hikes can be taken from these campsites. Those seeking more peace and quiet might be well-advised to cross into Jasper National Park and camp at the Adolphus Campground.

For most people, this is an in-and-out hike, requiring hikers to return along the same route that they came. The alternatives are a week-long hike over the North Boundary Trail (see Route IV below), that leaves hikers a long distance from where they started, or a hike over Moose

Pass and down the Moose River, which does not have a well-defined trail and is suitable only for very experienced hikers with good route-finding skills (see Route III below). Staff at the information desk in the Visitor Centre can provide information on hiking and camping in Mount Robson Provincial Park, and should be consulted before starting out. The ranger stations along the way can provide radio contact with the Visitor Centre in case of emergency.

Other than the large number of visitors, the only downside to hiking the Berg Lake trail and camping at the base of Mount Robson might be the weather. The highest mountain in any given area often traps passing clouds, leading to more rainy and overcast days than there might otherwise be. Having said this, I have hiked this trail four times, all in stunningly beautiful weather.

There are extensive gravel flats on the Robson River just south of Berg Lake, shown here, and again north of Kinney Lake. In between is the spectacular Valley of the Thousand Falls. The glacier-draped western side of Mount Robson can be seen in this image.

Trail Guide

Distances are adapted from existing trail guides: Patton and Robinson, Potter and Beers. Distances intermediate from those given in the sources are estimated from topographical maps and from hiking times. All distances are in kilometres.

From the Fraser River to Robson Pass and the Moose River trail junction along the Robson River

Maps   83 E/3 Mount Robson

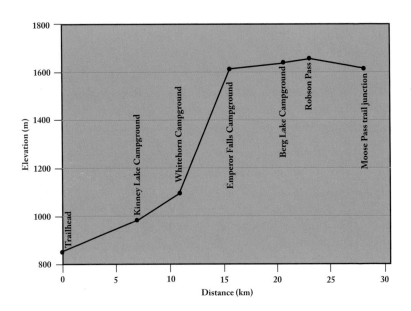

Trailhead

Follow the Yellowhead Highway (Hwy 16) 81 km west from Jasper to the Mount Robson Visitor Centre. A paved road (Kinney Lake Road) leads 2 km north from the service station to the Berg Lake trail parking area. The north end of the trail can be accessed along the Moose Pass route (Route III, pages 147–151) and the Snake Indian River trail (Route IV, pages 183–189) below.

0.0	Robson River bridge. The trail follows an old road along the Robson River, then climbs steadily through the forest, keeping close to the river.
4.4	Kinney Lake outlet bridge. Just across the bridge is a picnic area. The trail switchbacks steeply over a headland along the lake, then descends to lake level on a wide, well-groomed track.
6.9	Kinney Lake Campground. The bike rack at the end of the cycling trail is just beyond the campground. The trail splits here with a horse trail going left (west) onto the gravel flats. The main trail follows the side of the gravel flats, then climbs a high ridge. It drops to river level with switchbacks before crossing two bridges over branches of the Robson River.
8.6	Bridge across the Robson River. Emerge on an alluvial plain at the head of Kinney Lake. The plain has a bowl-like feature and great views of the mountains all around.
9.1	Bottom of Whitehorn Hill and an old, decommissioned campground. Begin a steep climb, initially through a forest, then through a deep, rocky gorge, and cross a small stream on a bridge.
10.9	Robson River suspension bridge. There is a ranger cabin on the left (west) and the Whitehorn Campground and picnic shelter on the right (east). Continue ahead through the campground towards a sheer rock wall with glacial streams pouring down it. The trail follows a flat section along the river.
12.0	Robson River bridge. The trail continues to climb steeply.

12.5	White Falls Viewpoint. The trail climbs steeply through the woods away from the river.
13.6	Falls of the Pool Viewpoint. The trail continues along the top of a deep gorge with the river far below. The next waterfall is visible in the distance.
15.0	Junction. Emperor Falls is to the right (east), 200m. Continue ahead (north), cross a deep gully on a bridge, continue the unrelenting uphill and climb a set of stairs. After the top of the stairs, the trail levels out, passes through an open forest and returns to river level.
15.6	Emperor Falls Campground. The trail proceeds along a wide, flat valley dominated by views of glaciers descending right to the river's edge. Cross a rockslide at the edge of the river flats and proceed to a giant alluvial fan at the head of Berg Lake.
18.1	Hargreaves Creek bridges. Cross the braided creek on a series of bridges along the alluvial fan.
18.5	Marmot Campground. The trail follows the shore of Berg Lake.
18.8	Junction. Hargreaves Lake to the left (west). Continue ahead (northeast) for Robson Pass, following the shore of Berg Lake.
20.6	Berg Lake Campground. The trail continues parallel to the lakeshore, passes the Hargreaves Shelter, crosses several bridged streams and proceeds along the edge of a large gravel flat.
21.6	Rearguard Campground.
22.0	Junction. Snowbird Pass is to the right (east), Berg Lake Ranger Station to the left (northwest) and Robson Pass ahead (northeast). The gravel flats become more treed.
22.6	Robson Pass Campground and Mumm Basin on the left. Continue along a very flat trail.
23.0	Robson Pass, Continental Divide and Jasper National Park boundary. The trail proceeds north along the flat Robson Pass area.
23.8	Adolphus Lake. The trail now enters the forest along the lake and

passes the end of the lake, where the trail splits with hikers going to the left (northwest) towards the Moose Pass junction.

25.6   Junction. Adolphus Campground and horse camp on the left (west). Proceed along a long meadow-like area with excellent views of the surrounding mountains.

26.0   Warden cabin on the right (east). The trail continues along the flat terrain.

26.7   Junction. A trail to the horse camp goes to the left (west). The flat trail enters a narrow valley, follows the lake's outlet stream, then starts to drop through light forest. The broad gravel flats of the Smoky River can be seen to the north.

28.4   Junction. The trail to Moose Pass goes to the right (northeast) (trail guide, page 151). The North Boundary Trail to Snake Indian Pass is straight ahead (north) (trail guide, page 189).

The author refreshes himself in the Robson River after seven days on the trail and before the final push to the parking lot.

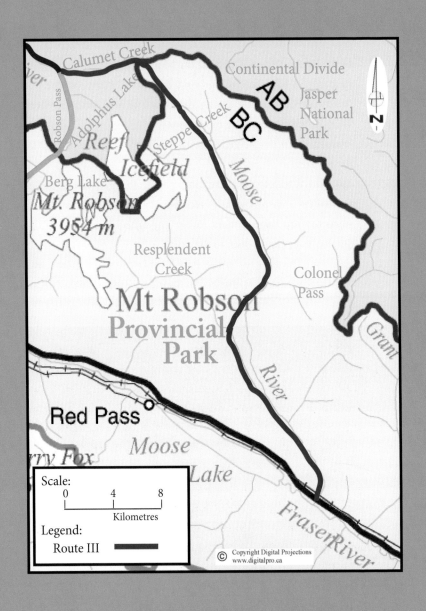

Calumet Creek

Continental Divide

Jasper National Park

AB

BC

Robson Pass

Adolphus Lake

Steppe Creek

Reef Icefield

Moose

Berg Lake

Mt. Robson 3954 m

Resplendent Creek

Colonel Pass

Mt Robson Provincial Park

River

Grant

Red Pass

Moose Lake

rry Fox

Fraser River

N

Scale:

0   4   8

Kilometres

Legend:

Route III

ROUTE III

Marshes and Fords: The Coleman-Moberly Route from the Fraser River to the base of Mount Robson via Moose Pass

I began preparing for the lengthy North Boundary Trail hike by completing several hikes in the Jasper area while my wife Cheryl was still there to take me to trailheads and pick me up at the end of the day. I then drove the rough – and at times intimidating – one-way Celestine Lake road and left Cheryl to repeat the difficult drive back to Jasper and on to Canmore alone while I set out on foot towards the Yellowhead highway *via* the Snake Indian River. The several day hikes I had completed before embarking upon the long hike soon began to take their toll. Before long, I was feeling tired rather than refreshed when I awoke in the morning. I began to question my plan to finish the hike on the challenging and poorly defined trail down the Moose River. On those rare occasions that I met someone on the trail, I enquired about the Moose River route; none had hiked it. One European couple did indicate that an American couple I would soon encounter had just completed the Moose River route. With this encouraging information, I carried on.

As predicted, I soon met up with the American couple. They were taking a day of rest after five days slogging up the Moose River route. They intended to spend most of the summer on the trails north of Mount

Robson and were proceeding slowly, carrying very large, heavy packs. When I asked if they thought my plan to hike the Moose River route in two days was feasible, they discussed the difficulties, took some time to consider my plan and exchanged a few whispered words before finally pronouncing their conclusion: no, they did not think my plan achievable. Because I was feeling tired and was anxious to complete my trek, I subconsciously welcomed the experienced hikers' conclusion. If I were to attempt the Moose River route and not finish it in the prescribed time, I would have no way of contacting Cheryl, who would be waiting for me at the trailhead and would initiate a needless search and rescue operation. I decided to abort my original plan and retrace my week-old footsteps down the well-maintained Berg Lake trail.

The new plan meant that I would arrive at the Mount Robson Visitor Centre a day early. After crossing into Mount Robson Provincial Park, I spotted a ranger station a short distance off the trail and decided to stop. The rangers informed me that they had radio contact with the Visitor Centre and would be happy to ask the attendants to phone my wife and ask her to meet me a day early. I then proceeded to hike to the Visitor Centre and spread out my camping gear on the lawn to dry as I awaited Cheryl's arrival. By evening my tired body was comfortably resting in my own bed, my thoughts only somewhat unsettled by the knowledge that I would still have to hike the Moose River route at some time in the future.

Fireweed following a recent fire on the Moose River trail.

CHRONOLOGY

1908   The Coleman brothers and the Reverend George Kinney hire John Yates of Lac St. Anne to provide the outfit and Adolphus Moberly of Jasper to guide them up the Moose River to Mount Robson. They do not succeed in climbing the mountain.

1909   Kinney and guide Curly Phillips take the Coleman-Moberly route up the Moose River, over Moose Pass and down the Smoky River to Berg Lake. They succeed in climbing Mount Robson.

        Arnold Mumm, Leopold Amery, Geoffrey Hastings, A.G. Priestly and Swiss guide Moritz Inderbinen hire John Yates to outfit and guide them along Moose River to Mount Robson. They do not succeed in climbing the mountain.

1910   Mumm returns with fellow climber J. Norman Collie and Swiss guide Moritz Inderbinen. Outfitter John Yates guides them along the Coleman-Moberly trail up Moose River to the base of Mount Robson. They are unable to climb the mountain.

1911   A.O. Wheeler, president of the Alpine Club of Canada, organizes a joint Canadian-American scientific expedition to the Mount Robson area. They follow the Coleman-Moberly trail to Moose Pass, down Calumet Creek to the Smoky River and on to Robson Pass.

        Conrad Kain and Curly Phillips take a pack train up the Moose River. After establishing a headquarters on the upper Moose, they proceed over Moose Pass, build a cabin and spend several months trapping and exploring on the headwaters of the Smoky, Moose and Beaver rivers.

1912   After the 1911 scientific expedition, Dr. Charles Walcott returns to the area with his son Sydney, Harry Blagden, and family cook and camp manager Arthur Brown. They head up the Coleman-Moberly trail along the Moose River and set up a permanent camp near Berg Lake.

Curly Phillips takes George D. Pratt and Phimister Proctor of New York hunting in the area he had trapped the previous winter.

1913   Walcott returns to the Berg Lake camp with his three surviving children. They spend four days reaching Berg Lake along the Moose River trail, with stops along the way to collect fossils and take scientific photographs.

Curly Phillips and Frank Doucette build a trail up the Robson River between Kinney and Berg lakes, eliminating the need for mountaineers to take the longer and more difficult trail up the Moose River.

Following the ACC camp at Mount Robson (see page 98), Lawrence Burpee engages outfitter Fred Stephens to take his party into Moose River country. They proceed towards Moose Pass and continue down the Moose River until they reach the railway and are able to catch a train back to Jasper.

1913   The federal government and the governments of Alberta and British Columbia commission surveys to delineate the inter-provincial boundary with official markers.

1914   Mary Jobe, Margaret Springate and guides Curly Phillips and Bert Wilkins travel up the Moose River and over Moose and Robson passes to Berg Lake. They return back over Robson Pass and down the Smoky River to Chown Creek and Bess Pass.

Famed Group of Seven artist A.Y. Jackson takes the new Berg Lake trail to Berg Lake. While there, he takes a side trip to Moose Pass.

1924   Jackson returns to the Mount Robson area, this time with fellow Group of Seven painter Lawren Harris. Details of this trip are sketchy, but it is clear that they painted in the area between Berg Lake and Moose Pass, probably having used the Kinney Lake trail to reach Berg Lake.

1928   Caroline Hinman travels up the Moose River with Lillian Gest and 13 other paying guests. After crossing the river many times, they reach Moose Pass and proceed to the old ACC camp near Robson Pass.

1929   Wildlife and landscape artist Carl Rungius arrives at Robson Station to meet two of outfitter Fred Brewster's men. They escort him on a five-day trip up the Moose River. Rungius returns to the area the next two summers.

Resplendent Creek on the Moose River trail.

HISTORY

MOUNTAINEERS

Having decided that Mount Robson would make a fitting inaugural climb for the Alpine Club of Canada, President Arthur Wheeler proceeded to ask the Coleman brothers to make the attempt. In the summer of 1907, they and their climbing companion, the Reverend George Kinney of Victoria, unsuccessfully attempted to reach the mountain by following the obvious route along the Robson River (see Route II above, pages 89-91).

The following year, the trio headed to Edmonton and proceeded west (approximately 67 km) to Lac St. Anne, with renewed determination to reach Mount Robson. This trip differed from their previous attempt in two significant ways. First, rather than providing their own outfit and engaging only a packer to help them with backcountry chores as they had on all previous trips in the mountains, the Colemans hired outfitter John Yates of Lac St. Anne to provide the outfit. They left the Yates homestead on August 4. When they reached the Athabasca River, they stopped at the home of Iroquois Métis John Moberly where they obtained some supplies and – more importantly – engaged Adolphus Moberly to guide them up the Moose River and around behind Mount Robson to Berg Lake. This was the only time since their first pack-train trip in 1892 that the Coleman brothers hired a guide.

The following morning, John Moberly transported the men and their outfit across the Athabasca River by canoe, followed by driving the horses into the river to swim across. A short visit with Lewis and Suzette Swift ensued, allowing the party to obtain additional supplies. They continued on and two days later:

On Dominion prairie, Adolphus Moberly and his family, with some relations, joined us, being rather tardy in their start; and henceforth our cavalcade was most picturesque, the stylish

Adolphus riding ahead and a party of Indians, including men, women, children, and dogs, with a mob of ponies, following at their leisure behind. We camped at the South of Moose River, whose valley we were to follow into the mountains, Adolphus going off alone to select and blaze out the little travelled and poorly marked trail.[1]

The Moberly trail up the Moose River to Moose Pass and Mount Robson is rarely used. A faint trail can be discerned in the post-forest fire plant growth underfoot, and the cut deadfalls seen on the right of the photo give hikers confidence that they are indeed on the trail. The small yellow triangle in the tree towards the left rear of the photo is another trail sign. Good route-finding skills are required to hike this trail.

The route Adolphus Moberly chose began by zigzagging up a steep grade west of the Moose River canyon before returning to the river. The next day, the Aboriginal families remained at the riverside campsite while the men proceeded up the valley on a faint trail. After much chopping they reached a fork in the river. Though one branch (Resplendent Creek) led directly towards Mount Robson, Moberly wisely insisted on the other branch, which led around the mountain and did not terminate at an icefield. They followed the creek a short distance, then turned eastward. After crossing a low ridge, they returned to the main branch of the Moose River, which they followed for ten miles (16 km), almost to its headwaters. The following day was Sunday, so the party did not move camp.

In the afternoon, Adolphus Moberly set out on horseback with Kinney and Yates, ostensibly to follow the tracks of a grizzly. In actual fact, his objective was to point out the route to Mount Robson. When they returned, Moberly announced that he would be leaving as his family needed him to provide meat. Having almost reached their destination, the Colemans were not concerned. On Monday morning Adolphus mounted his powerful black pony and headed down the valley. According to Coleman:

> He was the most typical and efficient savage [sic] I ever encountered, a striking figure, of powerful physique and tireless muscles, and thoroughly master of everything necessary for the hunter in the mountains. His fine black horse was like unto him and quite ruled over our bunch of ponies, in spite of being a stranger among them. Mounted erect on his horse, with gay clothing and trappings, Adolphus was the ideal centaur, at home in the wilderness, and quite naturally dominated the little party of Indians who had been travelling with us, though he was not more than twenty-one, while Adair [of the other Native family] must have been thirty-five.[2]

Adolphus Moberly, an Iroquois Métis who lived in the
Jasper area, was known to be a tireless worker of powerful
physique and very knowledgeable about the area around
Yellowhead Pass and Mount Robson. He led outfitter John
Yates up the Moose River on the trail that approaches
Mount Robson from the east.

The four men continued up the valley – following the route that
Adolphus had pointed out – past tree line at 6300 feet (1920 metres) and
through a barren, rocky valley to the summit of Moose Pass. Theirs was
the first recorded visit to the pass, though it had undoubtedly been visited
previously by local Aboriginal peoples.

Beyond the pass, the valley turned west and suddenly dropped down
to the headwaters of the Smoky River (Calumet Creek), a tributary of the
Peace River that flows into the Mackenzie and on to the Arctic Ocean.
Following Moberly's instructions, the adventurers cut across a wooded
ridge to another branch of the Smoky. Finding that they had turned
too soon, they suffered through some difficult terrain before reaching

the desired stream. They followed the stream to a spot near where they intended to begin climbing.

Because the hour was late and they had been soaked earlier by a sudden thunderstorm, they ended the day's travels there, setting up camp and drying their clothing and blankets around a fire. The following morning's rain and mist soon turned to an all-day snowstorm. Their only travels the next day consisted of moving camp to a grove of spruce and balsam near the great glacier descending from Robson, where they would have a good supply of dry wood and protection from the elements. In spite of the weather:

> A more delightful and inspiring camp could not be imagined, and from our door we could look across to a fine row of mountains, rising perhaps to nine thousand feet, their peaks now and then standing dark against the sky when the clouds thinned. Between them small blue glaciers crept a little way into the gorges, below which was rock and dark timber, and then parkland where small coloured spots were the ponies feeding.[3]

The adventurers honoured their skilful guide by naming a small lake to the northwest Adolphus Lake. To the southwest was a much larger lake, which they named Berg Lake for the icebergs that broke off the Blue Glacier and floated in the lake.

Despite some initial optimism, rain continued to fall in the valley day after day – snow on the peaks. Each morning Arthur Coleman rose at 3:30 to assess the weather, only to return to his blankets when he could not see the top of Mount Robson. He spent his days studying the geology and surveying the immediate area; his brother and Kinney climbed some nearby peaks as weather permitted. Yates spent his time cooking, tending to the horses, playing with the dog and seeking out game. They made three collective attempts to scale the mountain but all were thwarted by the weather, as was Kinney's valiant solo attempt.

Adolphus Lake, seen here with early morning mist rising from the surface, is located just north of Robson Pass and east of the trail. The lake was named to honour Adolphus Moberly, the man who led outfitter John Yates and climbers Arthur Coleman, Lucius Coleman and Reverend George Kinney to Moose Pass and directed them to the base of Mount Robson. These four were the first non-Natives to cross the pass.

After camping 21 days at an elevation of 5700 feet (1737 metres) at the foot of Mount Robson, they were forced to admit defeat. They retraced their steps to Swift's ranch, where they arrived on September 17. Bolstered by the fresh bread Suzette baked and the potatoes Lewis dug, they persevered another nine days to Lac St. Anne.

Much discussion of a third attempt on Mount Robson punctuated their travels. It was agreed that Yates would supply the horses and the Coleman brothers fully expected to take part in the operation. But Kinney reneged on whatever arrangements he had made with the Colemans, setting out earlier the next spring than they were able to. When they learned that he was already well on his way to Mount Robson, they abandoned their plans.

Lewis John Swift (1854–1940)

Lewis Swift was born in Cleveland, Ohio on February 20, 1854. As a young man he set out for the West. He worked in mining camps in the Denver area and for a while drove a stagecoach from Bismarck, North Dakota to Deadwood, South Dakota. After many years in the southern mountain states, he turned up briefly in the fledging town of Calgary in 1888 before moving north to the less populated area around Fort Edmonton. Between Fort Edmonton and the thriving village of Lac St. Anne he met many of the Métis from the Jasper area. In 1890 he travelled west to the mountains with the prominent Moberly family. Not yet ready to settle down, Swift proceeded over the Yellowhead Pass and continued on to Mission Creek in the Okanagan, where he appears to have remained for the next two years.

By 1893 his wanderlust seems to have waned. Turning up in Jasper with a six-inch grindstone and a supply of trade goods, he occupied the only remaining building of the old Jasper House fur trading post, which had been abandoned a decade earlier. He spent the next two years trading, hunting, trapping and exploring the area. By 1895 he had decided to build his home under the Palisades, east of Jasper adjacent to a creek west of the Snaring River. He built a one-room log cabin and started growing potatoes, wheat for flour and oats for his horses, all the while continuing a small trade. He also made regular trips to Edmonton, on some of which he procured cattle, pigs and chickens.

Swift's 1897 trip to Edmonton had a special purpose: at the country home of his friends the Wylies, about half a mile (0.8 km) north of today's Jasper Avenue, Swift married Suzette Chalifoux, a Métis woman who described her origins as Cree, Sioux and French. She was living with the Wylie family at the

In 1897 Lewis Swift brought his bride, Suzette Chalifoux, to the area east of Jasper. For many years the family home was a landmark in the Athabasca valley, welcoming all who passed through. This image was taken in 1928, in front of their log home.

time of her marriage, and had a two-year-old son, Albert Norris, born out of wedlock.

The Swifts were a compatible couple who worked together to develop the homestead. They raised horses and cattle and cleared land to grow grain and vegetables, irrigating their crops with water from the small stream nearby. The stream was also put to use driving an ingenious water-wheel that powered a grist mill to grind their own flour. Swift made all the family's furniture, constructed a one-horse cart using discs sawn from the end of a large Douglas fir tree for wheels, and was an accomplished blacksmith.

Lewis Swift was a creative pioneer who built this water wheel to power the grist mill he used to grind grain. This image was taken in 1909 when a survey crew was working in the area. Another of his innovations was to use cut sections from a large Douglas fir tree as wagon wheels.

The Swifts had two daughters, Lottie and Ida, and a son, Dean, born between 1899 and 1902. A fourth child, James, born in 1904, was fatally shot by 11-year-old Albert while the family was visiting Edmonton in 1906. Albert was sent to live in Fort Assiniboine with Suzette's sister and did not return to the family until 1930. Another son was born in 1907.

On September 14, 1907 the Government of Canada set aside Jasper Forest Park. Once the park boundaries had been established in January 1910, Lewis Swift was appointed the park's first game guardian. His duties were to patrol the park to prevent fires and protect game, which he continued until 1914- in spite of an ongoing dispute with park officials. At the same time as Swift was appointed game guardian, the government set about removing the so-called squatters who had been living in the park. Records indicate that seven Métis families (including the Swifts), were operating farms in the area. There were also other self-reliant individuals of Métis, Cree, Stoney and Iroquois origin who lived off the land. All except the Swifts came to terms with officials and agreed to move. The Swifts refused.

Lewis Swift had already demonstrated his determination to remain on what he considered to be his land when Grand Trunk Pacific Railway surveyors attempted to run a line through his house in 1908: he held them off at gunpoint for three days until the surveyors agreed to move the line. His resolve was not diminished by the passage of time. In August 1910 Swift went to Edmonton to successfully argue his rights; on September 18, 1911 he obtained title to the 160 acres surrounding his buildings. The property – the only freehold land in the park – became a bone of contention with park officials, but Swift simply refused to sell.

Some 16 years later, government officials offered $6000 in another attempt to buy out the Swift family, but times had been good and Swift refused the offer. A few years later, during the Depression, the Swifts decided to accept the offer and move to Jasper. Now it was the government's turn to stall, perhaps hoping to get a better deal. In 1935 Swift circumvented the government, selling to the Wilby family from England for $8000. He moved to Jasper, where he died in March, 1940. His widow died there in late 1946.

Lewis and Suzette Swift became legendary in the annals of exploration and settlement in the Jasper area. Their place soon became known as Swift's Place, a spot where visitors were always welcome and could be certain of a helping hand if needed. Travellers could often get badly-needed supplies, including fresh potatoes, milk and eggs – not to mention Mrs. Swift's fine needlework. Swift Creek, 21 kilometres northwest of Grande Cache, where many of the Jasper Métis went to live after eviction from the park, was likely named in his honour. Considering that Arthur Wheeler saw fit to name a mountain after the ne'er do well parasite, Mr. O'B, (see Eugene Francis O'Beirne biography above, pages 44–47) it is amazing that no one has seen fit to name a landmark in the Rockies after Lewis and Suzette Swift.

Kinney's fortuitous meeting with Curly Phillips and their trip to the mouth of the Moose River is described in Route I above. Kinney and Phillips retraced Kinney's year-old footsteps over the Coleman–Moberly route up the Moose River, over Moose Pass and down the Smoky River. On July 24 they continued past Berg Lake to set up camp in a small meadow near the Robson River at the foot of the northwest face of Mount Robson. Never had a climbing party faced a major climb so poorly equipped or so short of food, yet against all odds, they claim to have reached the summit.

Although this is not a book about climbing, Kinney's Mount Robson climb deserves some comment. For four years after the climb, Kinney was revered by the mountaineering community. Then Arthur Wheeler, president of the Alpine Club of Canada, set about quietly discrediting it. Over the years, writers have consistently downgraded Kinney's efforts, saying that he did not quite reach the summit of Mount Robson. But public opinion seems to be shifting. In 1998 Canada's eminent mountaineer and writer, Chic Scott, wrote:

> To me it's important that George Kinney now receive just recognition for his incredible accomplishment. Mount Robson towers 10,000 feet above the valley floor and modern mountaineers agree that Robson's snow-covered summit changes year by year. Some years there is a summit dome or snow-mushroom on the peak and other years there is not. It seems to be splitting hairs to discredit Kinney's great achievement over 60 disputed feet of snow.[4]

Similarly, mountaineer, lawyer and writer Bruce Fairley writes: "although the evidence is thus not completely beyond any doubt, I maintain that George Kinney should be credited with the first ascent of Mount Robson."[5] It seems somehow fitting that Kinney's name is known to almost all of the thousands of people who take the Kinney Lake to Berg Lake trail each summer, whereas the climbers who made the second ascent in 1913, which Wheeler claims to have been the first ascent, are known only to a small handful of devoted mountaineers.

Kinney's purported reason for not waiting for the Colemans before heading to Mount Robson in the spring of 1909 was that a group of experienced foreign climbers were heading towards the mountain and would get there before the combined Kinney-Coleman team could make it. The group from the Alpine Club (London) was made up of Arnold Mumm (of French champagne fame), Leopold Amery and Geoffrey Hastings, with Hastings's friend A.G. Priestly and Swiss guide Moritz

Inderbinen. John Yates of Lac St. Anne (who had outfitted the Coleman team the previous year), had been hired to outfit the Mumm group (see Route I above, pages 69–70) for more details of this trip). While being ferried across the Athabasca in John Moberly's canoe, the British party met Phillips and a very excited George Kinney who informed them they had just succeeded in climbing Mount Robson. The British party continued up the Moose River along the Coleman–Moberly route. Although they conducted a complete reconnaissance of the mountain, they were unable to climb it. Amery and Keeler, another member of the party, proceeded on foot down the Robson River, while the remainder retraced their steps down the Moose River route.

Mumm returned the following year with fellow climber J. Norman Collie and Swiss guide Moritz Inderbinen.[6] At the end of steel at Wolf Creek, east of the mountains, the trio met outfitter John Yates and helpers Fred Stephens, Allan Maconochie and George Swain, who had brought a large number of horses and two months' worth of supplies. They set out on July 18, crossing the Athabasca on the 26th and reaching Yellowhead Pass on the 29th. They proceeded up the Moose River on the Coleman–Moberly trail, now well-known to John Yates, though the only sign of the trail was the occasional blazed tree. They set up camp at the base of Mount Robson on August 9. By the 22nd they had given up on the idea of ascending the peak. Instead, they continued down the Smoky River and explored several side valleys. One of these exploration trips led them over an old Native trail to an easy pass into British Columbia, which they named Bess Pass. They continued on, looking for a pass to the east and a new route back to the Athabasca (see Route IV below, pages 160-164).

In 1913 Curly Phillips and Frank Doucette built the trail up the Robson River between Kinney Lake and Berg Lake, including the famous "Flying Trestle Bridge" (see Route II above, pages 98-99). After this trail became established, there was no longer any need for mountaineers to take the longer and more difficult trail up the Moose River and that route was left to others, mainly hunters and explorers.

Scientists

By 1911 A.O. Wheeler, president of the Alpine Club of Canada, had decided that he wanted to investigate the possibility of holding an ACC camp at Mount Robson. To this end, Wheeler organized an international scientific expedition to the area. The Canadian contingent consisted of Wheeler, a surveyor; Byron Harmon, the official ACC photographer; Conrad Kain, the ACC climbing guide; and the Reverend George Kinney, who had climbed Mount Robson in 1909. The American group was organized by Charles Walcott, head of the Smithsonian Institute, whose family had discovered the world famous Burgess Shale deposits. Walcott had also travelled widely in the Canadian Rockies, studying the geology and searching for fossils. He brought with him scientists Ned Hollister, J.H. Riley and Harry Blagden.[7] Their trip to the Yellowhead Pass is described above in Route II.

Arthur Wheeler, president of the Alpine Club of Canada (ACC), wanted both to assess the feasibility of holding an ACC climbing camp at Robson Pass and to do a scientific investigation of the area. The Canadian contingent consisted of (l–r) packer James Shand-Harvey, climber Reverend George Kinney, Swiss guide Conrad Kain and outfitter Curly Phillips with President Wheeler on the far right. The Smithsonian Institution scientists seated between Phillips and Wheeler are (l–r) Charles Walcott Jr., Harry Blagden, Ned Hollister and J.H. Riley.

The combined group completed a full circuit of Mount Robson, following the Coleman–Moberly trail up the Moose River valley to Moose Pass, then down Calumet Creek to the Smoky River and on to Robson

Pass. On their return, they walked down the Robson River to Kinney Lake where they were met by the pack train which had returned via the Moose River. As the large party proceeded, they conducted surveys and collected plant and animal specimens. Wheeler made the first topographical survey of the area and produced the first maps.

The following year, 1912, Dr. Charles Walcott and Harry Blagden returned to the area with Walcott's son Sydney, family cook and camp manager Arthur Brown of Washington, Closson Otto as outfitter and Doc Burgen as packer. The easterners took the train to Mile Seventeen west of Yellowhead Pass, the end of track, where R.C.W. Lett of the Grand Trunk Pacific Railway joined them for the next two weeks. The party's seven saddle horses and 11 pack horses headed up the Coleman-Moberly trail along the Moose River. Once they left the railway, they did not encounter another person until they returned to the track on August 24.

The headquarters for their summer's explorations was a permanent camp near Berg Lake. Sydney reported: "My father was busy every day on the geology of Robson and the surrounding mountains, and when he was not measuring the thickness of formations or searching for fossils, he was taking panoramic pictures of the area."[8]

Meanwhile, Sydney and Blagden were out hunting. Walcott reported to a Washington committee that:

Last year I sent an expedition to British Columbia into an area never hunted over by anyone, practically, connected with any American museum. That party found a new caribou, a new species, new type, the largest and most prominent one found. They also obtained other small forms. They were sent there more especially to get the typical goat, sheep, and grizzly bear of the Canadian Rockies. They succeeded in obtaining these specimens.[9]

The Otto brothers outfitted Walcott and his three children, Helen, Sidney and Stuart, for a return to the Berg Lake camp the following year.

Charles Walcott was accompanied by family members, friends and Smithsonian Institution (SI) scientists on his second trip to Mount Robson. He took this photo of (l-r): Sydney Walcott, Dr. I.F. Burgen (SI), Walcott's camp manager Arthur Brown, Harry Blagden (SI), R.C.W. Lett of the Grand Trunk Pacific Railway and outfitter Clossen Otto.

The Walcotts met the pack train on July 12, 1913 and spent four days travelling to Berg Lake along the previous year's Moose Lake trail, with stops along the way to collect fossils and take scientific photographs. With previous knowledge of the area and improved weather, Walcott's scientific efforts proved even more rewarding than those of the previous year. Towards the end of the month, Mr. and Mrs. Lett and Mary Vaux (Walcott's future wife) joined the ACC camp that had been set up between Berg Lake and Robson Pass and went to visit the Walcotts. Unfortunately, Mary had to return to Philadelphia early to attend to her ailing father. In mid-August, the Walcotts followed the Moose River route back to the railroad and the Letts's private rail car.

Between 1913 and 1924, the federal government and the governments of Alberta and British Columbia conducted surveys to mark the boundary between the two provinces. R.W. Cautley of the Dominion Land Survey set up camp near Moose Pass in 1922, with assistance from surveyors H.

J. Lambert and A.O. Wheeler (who had already completed a preliminary survey of the area in 1911). Because the ACC was holding a camp nearby, Wheeler decided to erect a special monument at the summit of Robson Pass. An impressive unveiling ceremony was held on July 31, with the towering Mount Robson as a backdrop and a crowd of picturesquely garbed mountain climbers assembled about the monument.[10]

HUNTERS AND TRAPPERS

Although several adventurers visited the Berg Lake area early in the twentieth century, the area north of Mount Robson remained virtually untouched – except by the hunters who were drawn to the wild nature of the country. Curly Phillips first came to the area in 1909. In 1911 he was the principal outfitter for the scientific expedition to the Mount Robson area that Conrad Kain attended as official ACC climbing guide. That winter, Kain and Phillips spent several months trapping and exploring on the headwaters of the Smoky, Moose and Beaver rivers. They took a pack train up the Moose River, set up headquarters on the upper Moose, then took the pack train over Moose Pass to build a cabin half-way between their headquarters and the Smoky River. They thought they had discovered Bess Pass that winter only to learn later that Collie and Mumm had already been there. They then worked their way down the Smoky to Chown Creek, which originates near Bess Pass, and Kain proceeded as far as Twin Tree Lake (see Route IV below).[11]

In September 1912 Phillips took hunters George D. Pratt and Phimister Proctor of New York into the area where he had set his trap line. Phillips and his packer Frank Doucette prepared for the outing by taking a pack train of 18 horses up the Moose River and over the pass to a teepee they had set up on the Smoky River. Doucette stayed behind with the supplies while Phillips herded the horses back over Moose Pass to the railway. He met his clients and another guide, John Yates, on September 10. Within three days, all the travellers and their luggage were in camp. They stayed until October 4, when they packed up and took the Coleman–

Moberly trail back to the railhead.

EXPLORERS

The 1913 ACC camp at Mount Robson brought together a large number of like-minded people eager to explore the area. At the same time another explorer – author, historian and librarian Lawrence Burpee – passed through on his way to Moose Pass. Burpee, like many others, walked from Robson Station to the ACC base camp on Kinney Lake. The following morning his party continued into the Valley of the Thousand Falls and on to the main ACC camp beyond Berg Lake, where they spent a pleasant evening on the lakeshore with the climbers.

But their ambitions did not stop there. The Burpee party had engaged outfitter Fred Stephens to take them into the Moose River country. Burpee felt that "of all trail guides in the Canadian Rockies none is the superior of Fred Stephens, whether as guide, philosopher or comrade. We who had heard his praises sung by others, congratulated ourselves when we learned he was to take us through the Moose River country."[12]

The next morning the 13-horse party trotted through the ACC camp, waving a reluctant good-bye. They followed a stream to Adolphus Lake, then Calumet Creek towards Moose Pass. Burpee exclaimed:

> Near the summit of the pass [Moose Pass] we found ourselves in the midst of one of the most exquisite of Alpine meadows. Imagine a great bowl of dark rock relieved here and there by patches of fresh snow, and at the foot of this bowl a soft emerald carpet, the green almost hidden by glowing patches of flowers, asters and arbutus and harebell, purple and white heather, lady's tresses and columbine, moss campion, the twin flower and the forget-me-not.[13]

After crossing the pass to British Columbia, the joy of the floral meadows was replaced by "mile upon mile of muskeg, where as we floundered slowly ahead we alternately admired Fred Stephens' unerring skill in following a trail that only became faintly visible for a foot or two every three or four hundred yards, and dammed him heartily for leading us into such a slough of despond."[14] The party continued down the Moose River, eventually reaching the railway line where they caught a train back to Jasper.[15]

Mary Jobe, a New York school teacher who loved exploring in the mountains, was one of the participants in the 1913 ACC camp that Burpee visited. She was so intrigued by the area that the following year she hired Curly Phillips, whom she had met at the camp, as guide and outfitter for a summer of exploration north of Mount Robson. Jobe's companion, Margaret Springate of Winnipeg; a second guide, Bert Wilkins and eight horses completed the party.[16]

On July 30 they set out into the horrible muskeg Burpee described along the Moose River. They continued over Moose and Robson passes to Berg Lake, returned over Robson Pass and followed the Smoky River to Chown Creek and Bess Pass. They continued travelling northwest, proceeding slowly and often with great difficulty through rough and untracked country, to eventually end up at the base of "Mount Kitchi" (Mount Sir Alexander). Jobe and Phillips made an unsuccessful attempt to climb the mountain before returning to the railroad via Moose River (see Route II above, pages 102-104, for additional Jobe–Phillips trips north of Mount Robson).

It could easily be argued, however, that the camp's greatest claim to fame was the fact that it served to introduce Caroline Hinman to the Canadian Rockies. Hinman went on to found Off the Beaten Track tours, and took paying guests – mainly teenaged girls from the eastern United States – on long wilderness treks through the Rockies. She had been to the Mount Robson area twice on backcountry tours and returned again in 1928 accompanied by her friend and fellow backcountry traveller, Lillian Gest, and 13 other paying guests.[17] Jim Boyce of Banff provided the outfit, with assistance from Charlie Hunter, Joe McCarthy, Ted McCarthy, Jack

LaCoste, "Hegie," Bert Mickel and Carl O'Kander.

The very large party started up the Moose River on July 3 and after innumerable river crossings reached Moose Pass on July 5. The following day they moved on to the old ACC camp near Robson Pass, where they took a typical two-day layover. They returned to Moose Pass on July 9, then continued down the Moose River to its junction with the Colonel Pass trail. They proceeded to head east over Colonel and Grant passes, eventually making their way to the Yellowhead Pass. The continuation of their trip saw them taking the steep Meadow Creek trail to the Tonquin Valley on July 16.[18]

Moose Pass is a high pass with relatively little tree growth near the top. The scenery is quite stunning; at the right time of the year, open meadows are filled with wildflowers. This image was taken near the top of the pass, looking south. Snow patches are still evident despite the fact it was the beginning of August.

ARTISTS

Very few early twentieth-century artists attempted the rigorous hike up the Kinney Lake to Berg Lake trail or the more demanding horse trail up the Moose River to Berg Lake. An exception was famed Group of Seven artist A.Y. Jackson, who hiked the newly-constructed trail through the Valley of a Thousand Falls in 1914.[19] While in the Berg Lake area, Jackson also visited Moose Pass, where he had a chance encounter with outfitter Curly Phillips. According to Jackson, "his first words were, 'What do you think about the war?' 'What war?' I asked". Then Curly told me that all Europe was at war, and that Canada was in it, too."[20] It seems that Jackson had not seen a newspaper for some time.

Jackson returned to the Mount Robson area in 1924, this time with Lawren Harris, another Group of Seven painter who would become perhaps even better known than Jackson, largely due to his paintings of the mountains.[21] Details of this trip are sketchy, but it is clear that they painted in the area between Berg Lake and Moose Pass, probably having used the Kinney Lake trail to reach Berg Lake.[22]

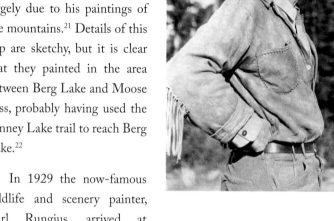

In 1929 the now-famous wildlife and scenery painter, Carl Rungius, arrived at Robson Station on the CNR.[23] As arranged, two of outfitter Fred Brewster's men promptly escorted him to a camp north of Mount Robson. He reported the five-day trip up the Moose River to be "one of the wildest and grandest mountain scenes I have ever observed" over a trail that was "one of the worst I have ever travelled."[24] Evidently the scenery more than compensated for the trail; Rungius returned to the area the following two summers.

Opposite: Lawren Harris, a member of the Group of Seven artists, made many trips to the Rockies to paint. His destinations included Mount Robson, Tonquin Valley, Maligne Lake and Lake O'Hara. He is seen here in 1946 standing in front of a painting by now-famous West Coast artist Emily Carr.

Above: Carl Rungius began painting in the Canadian Rockies when outfitter Jimmy Simpson invited him to accompany him on a backcountry trip in 1910. He subsequently travelled and painted widely in the Rockies and eventually moved to Banff.

The Trail Today

The Moose River trail's historical significance lies in its status as the original route to the base of Mount Robson. It is a difficult, wet trail that requires numerous river fords and creek crossings and considerable route-finding skills. I quickly decided that removing my boots at each ford and flooded meadow was not a viable option. The wet feet that resulted from simply wading through were well worth the discomfort.

Although there are some areas of outstanding beauty, the scenery as a whole is not spectacular. It is the swamps and fords, coupled with the periodic struggles to find the trail, that one tends to remember. For anyone wishing to test their route-finding skills and their ability to hike under less than ideal trail conditions, this is the place to be.

As I approached the top of the pass, the open meadows and wildflowers I passed through made the whole trip worthwhile. To top it off, I had the rare opportunity to spy a grizzly grazing on the open meadows. As it did not see me immediately, I was able to get some good photographs, albeit from a considerable distance. When the bruin did spot me, it simply ran a short distance farther away and continued with its repast.

Much of the route from Moose Lake up the Moose River to Moose Pass is memorable for its wet swamps, trail-finding difficulties and hazardous river crossings. My trip was made more pleasurable by the presence of a grizzly bear feeding on the abundant plant growth near the pass.

Trail Guide

Distances are adapted from existing trail guides: Patton and Robinson, Potter and Beers. Distances intermediate from those given in the sources are estimated from topographical maps and from hiking times. All distances are in kilometres.

From the Fraser River to Moose Pass and the Berg Lake trail junction along the Moose River

Maps   83 D/15 Lucerne

83 E/2 Resplendent Creek

83 E/3 Mount Robson

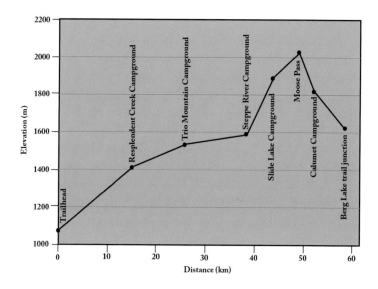

Trailhead

The Moose River trailhead is east of Moose Lake on the Yellowhead Highway (#16). Follow the highway 0.5 km west of the bridge across the Moose River or 3 km east of the Moose Lake boat launch. Follow the access road north to the parking area at the trailhead signboard.

Warning: This is not a trail as such. It is only suitable for experienced hikers who are skilled in route finding. Many people have lost their way on this route. Consider your options carefully before attempting it.

0.0   From the trailhead signpost, continue along the access road and cross the railroad tracks. Just after the "No Trespassing" signs, there is a sign saying "Moose River route." The trail leads off to the left (northwest). The trail initially climbs through a forested area, then drops down through a burned-out area, continuing on a bank parallel to the river.

3.6   Moose River. The trail continues along the river flats. The area is very open with good views of the surrounding mountains and snowfields.

6.9   The hiking trail swings to the left (west) to avoid crossing a side-stream and climbs a bank to avoid deadfalls. Yellow markers guide hikers back to the horse trail.

8.1   The trail runs parallel to a small lake on the left (west). Beyond the lake, the trail is faint. Watch carefully for cut trees and the occasional blaze. The route is essentially straight ahead (north).

8.7   Back to the main river. The route follows the riverbank through a burned-out forest that allows for good views of the surrounding mountains.

11.1   Resplendent Creek cascades. These are slightly upstream from the river. The trail turns left (west) and follows Resplendent Creek upstream, staying parallel to the creek, sometimes on a high bank above the creek. The creek becomes much wider and less turbulent. A sign says "2 km" over a tent symbol.

15.3   Resplendent Creek Campground. Ford the creek and continue on the east side, heading upstream on the gravel flats with no obvious trail. The route is indicated by occasional yellow markers; a large number of deadfalls make hiking difficult.

17.5   Near the end of the gravel flats, a spot clearly marked with flagging tape and metal markers has signs directing hikers to the right (east).

18.4   The trail leads away from the Resplendent Creek valley and crosses a low ridge in the forest. There are metal markers at the end of a swampy section, followed by a good horse trail and another swampy section with markers. What follows is a long stretch through a burned-out forest. There are some blazes in the trees, markers and flagging tape to mark the route, but cut deadfall is often the best guide. Come to a ridge just above the river.

20.1   Back at the Moose River. There is a yellow marker pointing upstream. The trail is indistinct but follows the river. Again, cut deadfalls are the best indicator of where the trail is, together with occasional metal markers.

21.7   Wooden bridge (marked 1990) across a tiny stream. Continue following the river until a yellow marker directs hikers into the forest. The trail soon returns to the river.

23.1   Rapids and small waterfalls on the river. The trail leaves the river and enters a burned out area with frequent metal markers, followed by a large marsh with metal markers and a faint trail. Return to the river and follow it upstream until metal markers direct hikers left (northwest) over a ridge into an unburned forest.

26.0   Trio Mountain Campground. From here, the horse trail goes to the right (east). There is no hiking trail; the pedestrian route continues straight ahead (north), well-marked with flagging tape and markers. It follows the river, crosses two large slide areas and reaches the edge of the forest, where more markers indicate the way ahead. From the markers, an easy-to-follow trail leads through the forest back to the river before leaving the river again, re-entering the forest, and then returning to the river.

29.5   A large marsh with a couple of metal markers but no obvious route across it. The best plan seems to be to keep to the right, ford a creek and return to the river, where there is a faint trail and yellow markers. Ford a small creek.

30.8   First Moose River ford. This is an easy ford with a yellow marker on the east side directing the way. Continue left (north) on the east side of the river through a marshy, open river valley. The trail enters the river flats. Watch for a marker on the far west side of the river.

32.4   Knee-deep ford to the west side of the river. The trail soon crosses a forested headland and returns to the river.

34.5   Ford the river to a marker on the east side. Follow the gravel flats north then enter the forest, continuing parallel to the river.

36.2   Ford to the west side of the river. The trail crosses another wooded headland, then drops down to Steppe Creek.

37.5   Ford Steppe Creek a bit upstream from the river. Continue through the woods to the creek and ford it again.

38.3   Steppe Creek Campground. After leaving the campground, ford Steppe Creek for the third time, then climb over a forested ridge to the northwest and return to the river.

40.6   Ford the Moose River to a metal sign on the east side. The trail starts to climb through the forest towards the pass. A sign in a tree shows a tent and says "2 km." The trail comes to a small meadow with a grassy ravine on the right (east) leading to the pass. Hikers should keep to the left (west) and not follow the ravine. There is a faint trail through the valley on the left. This is a spectacular area with glacial meltwater running down the sides of sheer mountains on the left (west).

43.8   Slide Lake Campground. The trail follows the high ground on the right, crosses open meadows filled with wildflowers, passes a rockslide and two small lakes, then reaches two rock cairns on either side of the trail. This is not, however, the top of the pass. From the cairns, the trail drops down to a small lake, then follows the east side of a stream through a broad open area with rolling hills and lots of flowers.

48.9   Moose Pass and national park boundary signs. There is a significant-sized stream, Calumet Creek, flowing west on the right (north). The trail continues through the meadows, gradually dropping into a forested area and following the bank of Calumet Creek.

51.9   Calumet Creek Campground. From the campground, the trail follows the creek's broad gravel flats. A ford is required near the end of the flat area, with metal markers directing hikers. The trail continues on a rough, rocky, wet section, often with dramatic views of the mountains to the right (north) and ahead (west).

56.7   Smoky River gravel flats. The trail continues parallel to (and often on) the gravel flats to the very fast-flowing and silt-laden Yates Torrent. The trail continues along the gravel flats (parallel to the Torrent), then climbs over a forested ridge.

58.0   Yates Torrent footbridge. After crossing the bridge, the trail goes downstream on the gravel flats, crosses to the left (west), then follows the Smoky River south.

58.3   Single log bridge across the Smoky River. The trail heads south, meets the horse trail and continues through the woods.

58.4   Junction. The North Boundary Trail goes to the right (north) (trail guide pages 183–189). The trail to Robson Pass and Berg Lake goes to the left (south). This is km 28.4 of the Fraser River to the Moose Pass trail junction along the Robson River (trail guide, page 117).

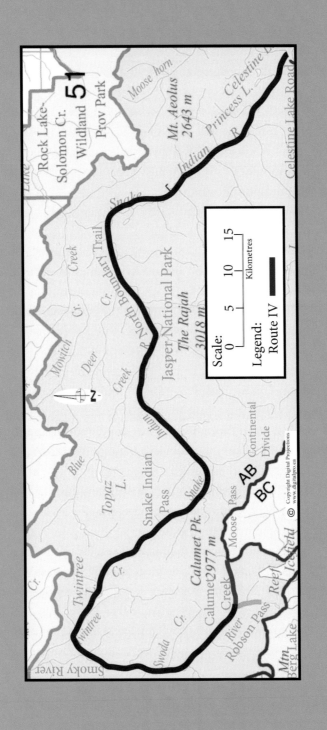

ROUTE IV

Peace and Beauty: The Mumm-Collie-Yates Route from Robson Pass to the
Athabasca River along the Snake Indian River (the North Boundary Trail)

The late August snowstorm was an inauspicious start to our hike up the Snake Indian River and over Snake Indian Pass. We were slow getting underway and had to camp outside a designated area. To compound the difficulties, we could not find a good place to hang our food away from a possible raid by hungry bears. The compromise was a spot well-protected from marauding squirrels. By morning the snow had ceased and our food supply was intact, allowing a much more optimistic group of six to set out on the trail. We soon found it to be well-maintained, with bridges over most streams and campgrounds featuring poles on which to store our food fastened between two trees high above our heads. At first, we had trouble finding outhouses, but soon discovered that the "facilities" consisted of a pole fastened between two trees – much like the pole used for storing food away from animals, except in this case, the pole was only about two feet off the ground and had a hole dug immediately beneath it. The location was generally out of sight of the main camping area and was easy to locate once we knew what we were looking for.

One highlight of the trip took place at the Blue Creek trail junction. This beautiful area about halfway along the route to Mount Robson was obviously a back-country centre for the wardens who worked in the district. On these long and remote hikes, we found that warden cabins make good resting places and occasionally even had a warden present and therefore made a habit of stopping at them. The wardens we encountered were normally friendly towards our well-organized and mannerly group and provided us with useful information about the trail ahead. The young people – eager to avoid a bear encounter of any kind – were especially interested in learning where grizzlies had recently been observed. Information of this kind was especially relevant in this case as, on approaching the warden cabin, the front group spied a grizzly just across the Snake Indian River from the cabin. A good-sized young man, who was part of the group, wisely made himself appear even larger than he was by standing very erect and waving his hands in the air. Much to the group's relief, this motion achieved the desired effect and the bruin immediately departed without crossing the river.

Once the group was reunited and the excitement over the bear sighting had subsided, we spread out in front of the unoccupied warden cabin to relax and have a morning snack. On the front of the cabin hung a log book which hikers had been signing for many years. The young people in the group were having a good laugh by looking up comments made by fellow hikers on their birth dates – nearly twenty years earlier. The log book was not old enough to provide any insight into what hikers felt on my birth date! One young lady volunteered to add a message on our behalf. She began with the statement: "We are a group of five teenagers and one crazy dad" and went on to list the names and ages of the group members, graciously giving my age as "daddy age." Sadly, when I hiked the trail nearly two decades later, the log book had disappeared without a trace.

Author Janice and her friends taking a break on the North Boundary Trail. The young lady sitting on the grass is preparing to write in the log book that was then kept at the cabin.

CHRONOLOGY

– 1800   Stone points and artefacts found near the mouth of the Snake Indian River indicate that the site was used several thousand years ago.

1821   Hudson's Bay Company traders attempt to establish a route along the Snake Indian and Smoky rivers. Many Iroquois, Métis and other Aboriginal hunters winter at various places along the route and travel to Jasper House to trade.

1825   Botanist Thomas Drummond hires an Aboriginal hunter to guide him to an old fur trading post on the Smoky River. They set out along the old Native trail up the Snake Indian River. After some forty miles, the snow becomes too deep to proceed. They turn east and north, eventually reaching the Berland River, where Drummond spends the next several months.

1896   Another young biologist, John Alden Loring, hires the Noyes family as outfitters. They set out along the Snake Indian River and cross the watershed to the Smoky River, which they follow north to the Grand Cache River. Loring spends his time studying the birds and animals of the region.

1910   Mountaineers A.L. Mumm and J. Norman Collie decide to return home from the Mount Robson area by a new route with Swiss guide Moritz Inderbinen and guides John Yates and Fred Stephens. Local Aboriginal people had told Yates of a trail that would provide a new route back to the Athabasca over a pass between the drainage of the Smoky and Snake Indian rivers.

1911   Essentially the same group returns to Mount Robson, follows the Snake Indian River and continues on to the Smoky River and Chown Creek.

1912   Samuel Prescott Fay, outfitter Fred Brewster and assistant Beau Gaetz use the Rock Lake trail to access the Snake Indian River. They proceed along the river, over Snake Indian Pass and past Twin Tree Lake to the Smoky River, where they spend some time exploring.

1914   Samuel Prescott Fay returns to the area with Charles R. Cross, again outfitted by Fred Brewster. They follow the old Native trail along the Snake Indian River as far as Blue Creek, where they head north into what is today Willmore Wilderness Park. They return to civilization after five months of exploring and enjoying the wilderness.

1921   Caroline Hinman takes one of her Off the Beaten Track tours along the Snake Indian River. The group, outfitted by Curly Phillips, includes 11 paying guests and five assistants for a total of 18 people. This very large party reaches Jasper on July 20 and starts northwest along the Stoney (Snake Indian) River. They return to the train at Robson Station by crossing Robson Pass and proceeding down the Robson River.

1929   One of the last large parties of the decade – and perhaps the last of the very large parties to travel in the area – leaves Jasper on July 8. The party is made up of J. Gilmour, Dr. Mary Goddard Potter, Miss Helen I. Buck, Mr. Benjamin S. Comstock, Mr. Mortimer Bishop, Mr. Frank N. Waterman and Mr. Newman D. Waffi and is outfitted by Curly Phillips. They travel up the Snake Indian River and north into today's Willmore Wilderness Park. Eventually they reach the Smoky River and return to Jasper along the Robson.

History

The trail up the Snake Indian (Stoney) River and over Snake Indian Pass to Twintree Lake and the Smoky River and on to Berg Lake is today known as the North Boundary Trail. Part of its beauty lies in the fact that sections remain as untouched by human hands as when the first recorded visit was made in the early nineteenth century. Other sections have an extensive history of human use. In 1983 archaeologists found ancient stone points and artefacts near the mouth of the Snake Indian River that indicated three different periods of occupation. The first, which was thousands of years ago, remained undated at the time of writing. A second group of early people made stone tools and processed animals for food 1700 years ago at that same site. Aboriginal peoples again used the site 500 years ago.[1] At the time of first contact with Europeans (1811), a crude trail led up the Snake Indian River to the Smoky River and on to Fort St. John on the Peace River.

Fur, Flora and Fauna

In 1821, five years before first crossing Yellowhead Pass into what was then known as New Caledonia, fur traders from the Hudson's Bay Company began attempting to establish a route along the Snake Indian and Smoky rivers. At the time, many Iroquois, Métis and other Aboriginal hunters were wintering along the route, travelling to Jasper House to trade.[2] Only four years later, in 1825, a botanist from the second Franklin expedition chose to spend a year in the Jasper region. Wishing to spend the winter at a fur trading post on the Smoky River, Thomas Drummond hired an indigenous hunter and guide to show him the way. They set out along the old Native trail up the Snake Indian River. After some 40 miles (64 km), the deep snow had buried any thoughts of reaching the Smoky. The pair turned east and north, eventually reaching the Berland River, where Drummond spent the next several months.

He returned to Jasper House in April, where he connected with Jacques Cardinal, the Hudson's Bay Company man who looked after the company's horses in the Jasper area.[3] Their summer travels included spending some time at Rock Lake, just east of the Snake Indian River and today a popular entrance to the Snake Indian River trail. They proceeded over Snake Indian Pass to the Smoky River, where Drummond remained until the end of September, before returning to Jasper. That same fall, he crossed the Athabasca Pass with the fur brigades. He later returned to Jasper and by December 1826 was back in Edmonton with a long list of plants and mosses attesting to the success of the first botanical expedition in the Jasper area.[4]

During the first half of the nineteenth century, Britain's large botanical centres were sending botanists worldwide to collect plant specimens for their permanent collections. Thomas Drummond, the first to collect in the Jasper area, travelled widely over territory that had never before seen a European. Later explorers along the Snake Indian River seemed to be unaware of Drummond's travels.

Some 70 years later another young biologist, John Alden Loring, spent several weeks exploring along the Athabasca and Miette rivers (and side valleys along the route) as far west as the Yellowhead Pass (see Route I above, page 67). He returned the following year, 1896, again hiring the Noyes family as outfitters. They set out from Edmonton on May 25 and set up camp on the Maligne River. On August 20 they started along the Snake Indian River and crossed the watershed to the Smoky River, which they followed north to the Grand Cache River. All along the way, Loring studied the birds and animals of the region.

OLD NATIVE TRAIL

Just fourteen years later, in 1910, a group of mountaineers in the Mount Robson area decided to return to the railroad near Jasper by a new route. The party was made up of A.L. Mumm (son of the famous champagne vintner), companion J. Norman Collie and Swiss guide Moritz Inderbinen, with guides John Yates and Fred Stephens and helpers Allan Maconochie and George Swain (see Route III above, page 136). Local Aboriginal people had told Yates of an old trail leading over a pass between the drainage of the Smoky and Snake Indian Rivers that would provide a new route back to the Athabasca. No one in the group appeared to have any knowledge of previous trips by Drummond and Loring. The party, led by Yates, started down the Smoky River and turned up a valley that led to beautiful Twintree Lake. According to Collie:

> Yates, who is the best guide in unknown country I have ever met, by some unaccountable instinct refused to follow the valley to its head and turned up a side valley; two days later he proved to be right. For we crossed an easy pass [Snake Indian Pass] above tree-line on the old and well-worn Indian trail, descending on the other side into a beautiful valley down which a fine stream ran through the pine woods.[5]

By September 16 they were at the Athabasca, near the site of Jasper House. Although the route had been used previously by Europeans, this was the first well-documented trip.

John Yates was an outfitter who worked out of the Lac St. Anne area west of Edmonton. He led several trips up the Moose River to Berg Lake and seemed to have a sixth sense for route-finding in unknown country. He led the first well-recorded trip from the base of Mount Robson to the Athabasca River, using his uncanny abilities to turn up a side valley that led to Snake Indian Pass.

Essentially the same group was back the following year, with helper Swain being replaced by expert axeman J. Smith. On July 24 they began the slow process of making their way up the Snake Indian River. Seven days of onerous work were required to cut their way up the first 25 miles (40 km) of fallen and burnt timber. Once past this major inconvenience, Smith returned to Jasper and the remainder of the party continued along the river. At one point, they found an old weather-beaten inscription on a tree trunk that read: "Jack Grame and Archie Turnbull, May 20, 1895," evidence that others – probably trappers – had been there before.[6]

After reaching the summit of Snake Indian Pass on August 4, they set up camp for three days so that Collie could do some surveying. Collie's surveys required the packers to exert considerable effort to transport the heavy and unwieldy equipment along the trail and to the top of the mountains. In this case, the mountain used for the survey was named Mount Hoodoo in honour of Yates' plucky bulldog who had to be roped up the last 600 feet (183 metres). Unfortunately, the name was not retained.

Outfitter John Yates came upon the beautiful Twintree Lake on his first trip along the Snake Indian River. The name of the lake is derived from the trees on the small island seen in the centre of the image.

After completing the survey, the party travelled up the watershed between the Stony and Smoky rivers, where they spied a lovely lake tucked away between the mountains. The two small islands near the foot of the lake, each adorned with a solitary pine tree, inspired them to name it Twin Pine Tree Lake (today's Twintree Lake).

They continued on to the Smoky River and Chown Creek, which they followed to Bess Pass. The old Native trail they were following appeared to have once been an important route, but had not been used for 30 years or so. They returned to the Athabasca along the same route, arriving on September 15. They had travelled a distance of 250 miles (402 km) over 60 days, mapping out an area of at least 400 square miles (1036 square km). Most of the travel was through wilderness essentially untouched by human beings.

The Route North

The remoteness of the area along the Snake Indian River appealed to a number of early explorers seeking a true wilderness experience. In 1912, the year after the historic Mumm-Collie-Yates trip, explorer and mountaineer S. Prescott Fay left Hinton, Alberta on August 8. He travelled north through the foothills to Rock Lake and west on to the Stony (Snake Indian) River. Fay was outfitted by Fred Brewster, who was then located in Hinton but soon moved to Jasper. They were assisted by Beau Gaetz, with a string of seven pack horses and supplies for seven weeks. The excursion began with several days' exploration along the Snake Indian River valley. Fay explained that:

> Owing to the very warm days, the snow and ice of the glaciers were melting rapidly, causing the rivers to rise and flooding the meadows all along this valley, so that the effect was that of a long, serpentine lake of a beautiful greenish colour, in which the mountains and glaciers were reflected. The trail was extremely bad, necessitating endless chopping, because of the amount of fallen timber, – the usual after-effect in burnt-over country. The mosquitoes were also troublesome, but the beauty of this valley fully compensated for all our discomforts.[7]

Opposite: The beauty Samuel Prescott Fay found in the Snake Indian Valley is evident in this image. The valley's many broad meadows and lakes are surrounded by mountains, often – as in this case – with glaciers to enhance the view.

Samuel Prescott (Pete) Fay (1884–1971)

Pete Fay was born in Boston, Massachusetts on May 27, 1884 to a well-established New England family descended from a whaling magnate. Nothing is known of his early life except that his lifelong association with Martha's Vineyard was presumably initiated by spending much time there during his childhood and adolescence. He graduated from Harvard in 1907 with a Bachelor of Arts degree and started working as an investment counsellor. He first visited the Canadian Rockies in 1906; between 1906 and 1912 he climbed in the Lake Louise and Lake O'Hara areas at least three times. Unlike his cousin, Professor Charles Fay, he appears not to have documented his early forays into the mountains, so no descriptions of these trips remain.

Samuel Prescott Fay made Rocky Mountain history with his 1914 five-month wilderness expedition from Jasper north to Hudson's Hope on the Peace River. His exact route has never been duplicated in one continuous trip. Fortunately for lovers of wilderness travel, Fay kept a detailed diary which has recently been published.

Fay was more interested in hunting than in climbing, so when the completion of the Grand Trunk Pacific railway opened up the area north of Jasper, Fay was immediately interested. In early August 1912 he arrived in Hinton, Alberta to meet Fred Brewster, whom he had engaged to take him on an exploratory trip into the virtually unknown country north of Mount Robson and west of the Smoky River. The area was reported to abound in bear, deer, moose and goat, with the added attraction – not available further south – of caribou. Fay had expected to be back in Hinton by the end of September but bad weather, a shortage of food and an utterly unsuccessful hunt forced a change of plans. He and Brewster abandoned any thoughts of further exploration and headed to Hinton along a new route. Plagued by snowstorms, the exhausted party did not reach Hinton until the end of October.

Fay had made plans to return in 1913, but major surgery that winter rendered him unable to withstand the rigours of another trip into untracked wilderness. Instead, he agreed to Brewster's suggestion of a series of shorter trips that would be pursued at a more leisurely pace over the course of several months. They began with a few weeks in the Smoky River area north of Mount Robson, which they followed with several weeks hunting sheep in the Brazeau country and as far south as Lake Louise, and hunting caribou in the high country along the Great Divide near Fortress Lake. En route, plans for a much more ambitious trip the following year began to evolve.

These plans took on added dimensions when Fay decided to bring along a friend, C.R. Cross, Jr. of Boston, and when the Biological Survey of the US Department of Agriculture asked him to collect animal skins and report on the birds and mammals of the region. Fay's desire to explore the northern limit of the Rocky Mountain bighorn sheep range and the area around the "Big Mountain" named Mount Kitchi by Mary Jobe further extended the scope of the explorations.[8] The party left Jasper on June 26 and reached Hudson's Hope on the Peace River on October 15. This 1200 kilometre foray into largely untracked and unmapped wilderness was the longest such trip ever taken in the Rocky Mountains. While Fay hadn't kept a diary on his previous trips, he did so on this trip. After his return, he wrote several articles and the entire diary has recently been published as *The Forgotten Explorer: Samuel Prescott Fay's 1914 Expedition to the Northern Rockies.*

After learning that war had broken out in Europe, Fay volunteered as a driver with the American Ambulance Field Service in France and was cited for bravery. When the United States joined the Allies in 1917, Fay was commissioned as a lieutenant and served as an aerial observer with the 91st Aero Squadron.

Fay was a member of the American Alpine Club from the early years of the twentieth century to the end of his days. In his senior years, he also became interested in Arctic exploration and became a member of the Arctic Institute. Nevertheless, there is no record of any climbing or exploration after his monumental excursion of 1914. He maintained a lifelong friendship with Fred Brewster, evidenced in part by a 1940 family photo of the two of them in Jasper. Few other details of Fay's personal life are available, except that he married a woman named Hester and they had two daughters and a son.

Fay's health deteriorated towards the end of his life. He died at home in Chestnut Hill, Massachusetts on August 11,

1971, six months after his wife Hester. Fay's name is practically unknown in the literature of the Rocky Mountains, though Fay Lake, near Mount Sir Alexander, keeps his name alive in the northern wilderness. The 2009 publication of his diary will undoubtedly reawaken mountain adventurers to the huge contribution that Fay made to promoting further travel in the wilderness north of Mount Robson.

The party crossed Snake Indian Pass, which they named Marmot Pass due to the abundance of marmots, and went on to Twintree Lake:

So called because of two rocks in the middle, on each of which stands a solitary spruce. It is a beautiful sheet of water nearly two miles long, the colour of which is a soft green…Twin Tree Lake is set in a deep basin, surrounded by mountains of between 9000 and 10,000 feet [2743 and 3048 metres]. At its head is a green meadow, or muskeg, and the stream flowing in carries so much mud and dirt from above that quite a delta has been formed at its mouth…Altogether the composition of lake, mountains and glaciers is very delightful, suggestive as it is of peace and solitude.[9]

Their journey took them to the Smoky River, which they proceeded to explore. By the end of September they had reached the Kawka River. Their food supply was low so they headed for Hinton, attempting to find a route which would avoid the snow-covered high passes. They reached Hinton by the end of October with men, horses and food supply completely exhausted.

Two years later, Fay returned with Charles R. Cross, a Boston friend and neighbour. Fred Brewster, now of Jasper, outfitted the pair with assistance from Bob Jones and Jack Symes. The pack train of 16 pack

Above: Snake Indian Pass separates the drainage of the Snake Indian River, which flows east, from that of the Smoky River, which flows north. Although the pass is geographically close to Moose Pass, it is necessary to take a long circular route around Calumet Peak and Swoda and Wolverine mountains to reach Moose and Robson passes. Like many high mountain passes, Snake Indian Pass is meadow-like and sparsely populated with trees.

Opposite: The Ewan Moberly Homestead Historic Site on Moberly Flats is one of the interesting stopping places on the Celestine Lake Road en route to the Snake Indian River where the North Boundary Trail hike begins. The old house, shown here, has been preserved with a new roof, as evidenced by the freshly cut logs. The squared logs and dovetail corners of the original house reveal the Moberly's skilled axe work.

horses and five saddle horses left Jasper on June 26, 1914 with supplies for four months. Their intention was to explore north of Jasper as far as Hudson's Hope on the Peace River, scoping out the range of Rocky Mountain bighorn sheep. The adventurers travelled east along the west bank of the Athabasca River, (along today's Celestine Lake Road), passed Swift's homestead, crossed the Snaring River and camped at Moberly Flats, where log houses and graves served as a reminder of earlier Métis settlers. By noon of the following day they had reached the Stony (Snake

Indian) River, which they were able to ford without difficulty. "On the other side," Fay reported, "we at last were on a trail and away from the wagon road and it seemed as if the trip had really begun. We camped in a beautiful little flat covered with flowers, the purple blossoms of the pea vine and the red tiger lilies predominating."[10]

The next morning, they headed northwest along the river valley. They reached the trail from Rock Lake on June 30, then continued on the old Native trail along the Snake Indian River, looking for a fork in the trail where they would head north. As Fay explains:

> The upper Stony River is pretty country, fine rocky mountains with snow and ice on one side and fine-looking sheep mountains on the other. For a day the down timber is bad and country all

burnt, but fine, open green timber prevails. Goat ranges on one hand and sheep hills on the other, with moose and deer in the valley, as well as bear. We have been looking for a certain spot for two days where our trail forks but not until 3 p.m. did we find that we had passed it about twenty miles back...so tomorrow we will have to go back and return through all the down timber once more.[11]

They returned to Deer Creek, then headed north into today's Willmore Wilderness Park to the headwaters of the Sulphur River. They returned to civilization at Grand Prairie after five months of exploring and enjoying the wilderness.

The Fay group towards the end of their epic five-month wilderness trek. This image was taken at the Hudson's Bay Co. trading post on the Peace River. The group (l–r): Charles Prescott Fay, his friend Charles Cross, helpers Bob Jones and Jack Symes and outfitter Fred Brewster, are looking remarkably fit and hardy after such a long, and at times trying, trip.

Frederick Archibald Brewster (1884–1969)

Fred Brewster was born on December 21, 1884 in Kildonan, Manitoba, the third of John and Bella Brewster's seven children. In 1886 John Brewster moved to Banff and established a dairy. The family followed in 1888. Young Fred grew up in the pioneer town of Banff, attending the newly-built school and helping his older brothers with their outfitting business and his father with his very successful dairy business. He was sent to Winnipeg's St. John's College for his later schooling, completing his course in 1905.

Unsure of what to do next, Brewster accepted his Uncle George's invitation to accompany him on a combination horse and canoe exploration trip from Ashcroft, 160 miles (461 km) east of Vancouver on the Canadian Pacific Railway line, all the way to Edmonton via Peace River Crossing and Athabasca Landing. They arrived in June after nearly a year on the trail. Far from fatigued, Brewster promptly repeated the trip with family friend Fred Hussey in a mere three and a half months. This was Brewster's first real experience with backcountry horse travel; at its conclusion he felt he had had enough of trail life to last a lifetime. Little did he know to what extent this experience would determine his life's work.

First, however, Brewster turned his thoughts to more academic pursuits. In the fall of 1906 he enrolled in Queen's University and graduated with a degree in Mining Engineering three years later. During his university summers, Brewster prospected on Vancouver Island and the Queen Charlotte Islands for the Consolidated Mining and Smelting Company. After graduating, he returned to continue this pursuit on his own.

Fred Brewster, a member of Banff's prominent Brewster family, moved north and settled in Jasper in 1912. He mostly worked as an outfitter during his early years in Jasper but gradually expanded his business interests to become an influential and well-loved businessman. He was known by most simply as Major Brewster, a title earned during his war service.

Unsuccessful, he returned to Banff in the fall of 1909. He worked as a ranch hand and trail guide until the following year, when his brother-in-law Phil Moore suggested that the two of them and Fred's 17-year-old brother Jack form a company. Brewster and Moore initially worked out of Red Deer, freighting for a company building a rail line to the coal mining town of Nordegg. They soon moved the horses and equipment to the fledging town of Prairie Creek on the Grand Trunk Pacific line east of Jasper, where they constructed temporary corrals and put up tents as living quarters.

Work was plentiful but Brewster felt that outfitting would likely form the bulk of their future business and set out to become familiar with the country. He explored the area around Mount Robson and the Yellowhead Pass early in 1911, returning through the future site of Jasper. Following the lead of other outfitters in the region, Brewster and Moore moved their operation to Jasper in 1912 and built more permanent stables and corrals.

Brewster and Moore were very fortunate to have been contracted by explorer and hunter Samuel Prescott Fay for the summers of 1912 to 1914. These trips, each lasting several months, were led by Fred Brewster. On October 7, 1914, near the end of their five-month trip, the exploring party met a trapper who informed them that the First World War had been underway for two months!

That same year, Brewster and Moore were awarded a contract to cut a trail from Jasper to the south end of Medicine Lake. Having completed that work, Brewster joined the army, was commissioned as a Major in the Second Tunnelling Division and was sent overseas. He was subsequently awarded the Military Medal and Bar.

After the war, Brewster kept an office in New York, where he frequently travelled to promote his businesses. During one of these trips he met Azalia Adams, the daughter of famed American architect John Adams. They were married in 1924. The couple returned to Jasper, where Brewster built a house for his wife. Unfortunately she was not well and suffered a nervous breakdown in 1928. She was sent away to mental hospitals, first in New Westminster, British Columbia then in Verdun, Quebec, where she died in 1961. They did not have any children and there is no mention of Brewster's wife or his marriage in any of his papers – and virtually no mention of her in Jasper, in spite of Fred's key role in the town's history.

Even during the war, the Grand Trunk Pacific railway was attempting to attract tourists to Jasper. To this end, sleeping tents on wooden platforms and a large dining tent had been built on the shore of Horseshoe Lake (today's Lac Beauvert). The Brewsters (Phil Moore left the company in 1919) took over this camp in 1919 and greatly expanded it by adding a log kitchen and dining room. In 1922 they replaced the sleeping tents with log cabins. By this time, Jack Brewster had left the company to form his own. In 1923, Fred Brewster sold the rights to the camp (which became Jasper Park Lodge) to the newly formed Canadian National Railway but retained the rights to the outfitting and guiding business carried out from the site, which became the main thrust of his company.

His influence in the tourist trail-riding business increased in 1925, when he organized the Jasper chapter of the newly formed and very popular Trail Riders of the Canadian Rockies. By 1928 Brewster had expanded and refined his increasingly popular Maligne Lake circular tour and, with the help of the railway, added the Medicine Lake chalet as a half-way stopover. The tour now included a stay at Brewster's Maligne Lake Chalet, built in 1927, as well as a boat tour on the lake. Over the next several years, Brewster continually improved his existing tours and added more to his repertoire. He also added to his series of Rocky Mountain camps by building camps at Little and Big Shovel passes and Tekarra Basin as part of his Sky Line Trail

Rides and building Black Cat Ranch outside the park for hunting parties in 1935. When the Jasper Park Ski Club was formed in 1936, Brewster became an original member and president; some of his camps and chalets were used for winter trips. After outfitter Curly Phillips died in an avalanche in 1938, Brewster also obtained the boat concession at Maligne and Medicine lakes. He built the Columbia Icefields Chalet in 1939 and in 1941 added a backcountry chalet in the Tonquin Valley. During the Second World War, he assisted with the mountain warfare training of the Lovat Scouts, a group of Arctic-trained soldiers from Scotland. He sold most of these businesses in the 1950s, but continued to run his boat tours and outfitting business until his retirement in 1962.

Major Brewster, as Fred was commonly known, became a local legend. He was a founding member of the Jasper-Yellowhead Historical Society and a life member of the Jasper Park Ski Club, the Jasper Chamber of Commerce and the Jasper branch of the Canadian Legion. Titled the Gentleman of the Rockies, this soft-spoken and modest man chatted knowledgeably about his beloved mountains until he died in 1969 at age 85. He is buried in the Jasper cemetery next to his wife Azalia.

ERA OF LARGE PACK TRAINS

Once Mumm, Collie and Yates had made the Snake Indian River trail known to the backcountry travellers of the period, it was inevitable that Caroline Hinman would take one of her Off the Beaten Track tours along the route. Hinman had a party of 18 people: 11 paying guests, outfitter Curly Phillips, his five assistants and herself. The pack train consisted of 47 horses and 5000 pounds (2268 kilograms) of supplies and equipment, approximately 170 pounds (77 kilograms) per pack horse. This very large party assembled in Jasper on July 20, 1921 and started northwest along the Stoney (Snake Indian) River. They turned east at the trail to Rock Lake, then north into today's Willmore Wilderness Park, returning to the Snake Indian River valley via Blue Creek. They had layover days at Rock Lake and again on Hardscrabble River before returning to the Snake Indian River on August 11. From there they proceeded to Twintree Lake and the Smoky River, taking side trips to the Short River, Bess Pass and Moose Pass, with several layover days at interesting spots. Their homeward route was over Robson Pass and along the Berg Lake trail down the Robson River to the train at Robson Station, which they boarded on September 1.[12]

Other explorers made similar expeditions into the country north of Mount Robson during the 1920s. One trip in the summer of 1924 had a different twist. At the conclusion of the Alpine Club of Canada's Robson Pass camp, A.S. Sibbald, H.E. Sampson, G.A. Gambs and D.J.M. McGeary were taken by saddle horse and pack train (supplied by Curly Phillips) down the Smoky River and west to a suitable point between Bess and Jack Pine passes. They then took the unusual step of sending the horses back. Their first task was to set up a base camp, after which they spent several days exploring the area. From there they intended to backpack along a mountaineering route to Robson Station. They set out on August 2 and arrived at the station on the evening of August 13, having spent 12 days, including "some of the very finest and some of the most utterly cheerless which we had ever spent in the mountains."[13]

One of the last large parties of the decade – and perhaps the last of the very large parties to travel in the area – set out on July 8, 1929. The party consisted of J. Gilmour, Dr. Mary Goddard Potter, Miss Helen I. Buck, Mr. Benjamin S. Comstock, Mr. Mortimer Bishop, Mr. Frank N. Waterman and Mr. Newman D. Waffi with outfitter Curly Phillips, helpers Adam Joachim, David Moberly, Kenneth and Arthur Allen and cook Jack McMillan. Thirty-seven horses were required to carry the adventurers, their helpers and all the supplies Phillips was famous for taking to ensure the comfort of his clients. Their objective was to climb Mount Sir Alexander far to the northwest. They travelled up the Snake Indian River and north into the area of Willmore Wilderness Park, eventually reaching the Smoky River. It took them 14 days to reach the base of the mountain, which Waffi, Buck and Gilmore managed to summit. The party returned to Jasper along the Robson River.[14]

Andrew Sibbald's chance encounter with Hebert Sampson (l) in Saskatoon in 1916 set Sibbald's life on a new path. It was Sampson who introduced Sibbald to mountaineering. Always interested in trying new things, the pair hiked without horses through untracked country from Jackpine Pass back to Robson Station.

THE TRAIL TODAY

The most difficult part of hiking the trail from the Athabasca River to the Smoky River (the North Boundary Trail) may be arranging transportation at either end. Most people will want to start at the Celestine Lake Road. This road is a worthy challenge in itself. It can be traversed by most vehicles with care, but a high-clearance vehicle such as a van or SUV is a definite asset. The rough and rocky road is downright scary in places and both my wife, Cheryl, and one of Janice's teenaged friends expressed doubts about driving the road on their own after travelling it as a passenger – though after getting behind the wheel themselves both agreed that it was not as bad as it appeared. Along the way, a visit to the Ewan Moberly homestead makes a nice break.

An alternate route to the Snake Indian River is to drive through the foothills to Rock Lake, where a relatively short hike (14 km) takes one to the Snake Indian River. The main disadvantage of this approach is that, without back-tracking 11 kilometres, one misses Snake Indian Falls, the highlight of this portion of the trail. The authors have not used this route.

As hikers proceed there are many opportunities for side trips or loop trips from the Snake Indian River trail. These options include exploring Willow, Deer and Blue creeks or McLaren's, Bess, Carcajou and Moose passes, and continuing north along the Smoky River. Many of these options will lead into the Willmore Wilderness Park, a desirable destination in its own right.

Once across Snake Indian Pass, the route down Twintree Creek and especially past Twintree Lake continues the earlier experience of quiet beauty. After the end of the lake, the trail crosses a headland into the Smoky River valley and the scenery becomes much more rugged with the trail largely following the extensive gravel flats of the river.

Regardless of which side trips one chooses, most hikers will want to exit along the beautiful but very busy Berg Lake trail. After spending a week or more in the quiet beauty of the Snake Indian valley, the number of people in the area between Berg Lake and the Mount Robson Visitor Centre during July and August will be a shock to the senses. My group of Janice and her teenaged friends had made arrangements to camp in one of the many Berg Lake campgrounds but once there, no one wanted to stop, so we took advantage of the long summer days and pushed on to trail's end.

Snake Indian Falls (on the river of the same name) is one of the highlights of hiking the North Boundary Trail from Celestine Lake. This photograph of the falls with the author, Janice and her friends standing on a rocky ledge is one of my favourites.

The main alterative to the Berg Lake trail is the Moose River trail. This will be as quiet and peaceful as anyone could desire (see Route III above) but is an option only for experienced hikers who are skilled in route finding. It is a difficult trail with many river crossings and wetlands to negotiate. Because the trail ends at a remote area along the Yellowhead Highway, you will need to arrange transportation ahead of time. Hitch-hiking along this busy transportation corridor may be difficult or near impossible.

The North Boundary Trail is a well-maintained back-country trail with lots of campsites and bridges over most streams. It is peaceful river valley hiking with a charm all its own, the most outstanding feature being Snake Indian Pass. It is a truly wonderful backcountry experience for those seeking quiet beauty in the backcountry. A real benefit is the number of animals and birds in the Snake Indian valley. Many backcountry trails are fairly devoid of song-birds; for a solo hiker like me the musical chorus in the upper Snake Indian valley was a true delight. As I proceeded past some of the wetlands near the trail, it was easy to spot moose feeding on underwater plant life on the opposite shore. They were far enough away that even after they discerned my presence, they tended to move away only slowly, leaving lots of time to observe them from a distance.

This cow-calf pair of moose was quietly feeding on the side of a shallow lake in the Snake Indian valley before they caught a whiff of my scent. They slowly moved away into the forest, no doubt returning to their meal when any possible threat from me had passed. I espied scenes of this type several times when hiking through the valley.

My most interesting experience was a game of cat-and-mouse with a grizzly bear. While walking along the trail, I spotted a bruin some distance away, proceeding steadily along the end of the lake. It seemed fairly obvious that if the bear continued on its present course and I continued along the hiking trail we would cross paths some time ahead. Since I am always interested in photographing wildlife – and carry a telephoto lens for my camera – I took the camera out of its carrying case, turned it on and got it ready for a quick shot. I proceeded cautiously, camera in hand, keeping a careful watch in the direction that I expected to see the bear but saw nothing. Eventually I put the camera away, feeling that I had missed my chance for a photo. As Murphy's Law would predict, shortly thereafter, I encountered a large grizzly on the trail ahead of me. The bear behaved predictably for an animal in a remote area where it is unlikely to be habituated to humans: it took off through the woods and all that I saw after the first glimpse was a ball of brown fur hightailing it away from me. There was no time even to take the camera out of its bag.

Trail Guide

Distances are adapted from existing trail guides: Patton and Robinson, Potter and Beers. Distances intermediate from those given in the sources are estimated from topographical maps and from hiking times. All distances are in kilometres.

From the Athabasca River to the Moose Pass Trail Junction along the Snake Indian River

Maps   83 E/1 Snaring
83 E/8 Rock Lake
83 E/7 Blue Creek
83 E/6 Twintree Lake
83 E/3 Mount Robson
Gem Trek Jasper and Maligne Lake

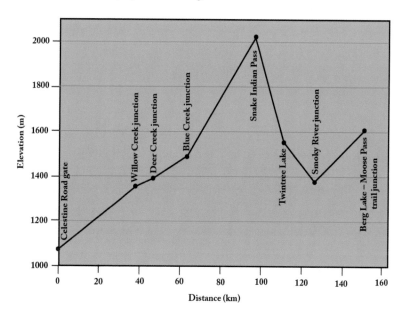

Trailhead

Although Mumm, Collie and Yates first explored the trail known today known as the North Boundary Trail from west to east, it can easily be travelled in either direction. We have provided a trail guide from east to west, as this will be the preference of most hikers. To access the east end of the trail, follow the Yellowhead Highway (Hwy 16) 9 km north of the Jasper townsite's north exit to the Celestine Lake Road. Turn left (west) and follow this initially paved, then gravel, road 13.7 km to a pullout near Coral Creek. Beyond here, the road is one-way, running on an alternating schedule. The schedule is posted at the beginning of the gravel section of the road. Follow the narrow and rocky one-way road to a locked gate and parking area at km 27.9, 0.5 km before the Snake Indian River bridge. The west end of the trail is at Robson Pass, km 23.0 of the Fraser River to Robson Pass along the Robson River trail, page 116.

0.0	Set out on an old road that drops down to the Snake Indian River.
0.5	Snake Indian River bridge. The trail continues along an old road that climbs steadily to the top of a bank: a pleasant walk through mixed forest.
5.2	Large parking area. This was the end of the Celestine Lake Road before the bridge was decommissioned for vehicles. A sign points to the Celestine Lake Campground on the right. The trail continues straight ahead (northwest), marked by a sign reading "Shalebanks Campground 12 km." The trail continues on the old road through the forest, with frequent views of the surrounding mountains ahead, then steadily drops into the Snake Indian River valley.
17.3	Shalebanks Campground. Cross a log bridge over a creek near the campground and re-join the old road.
21.2	At river level again. Start a gentle but steady uphill climb. The trail levels off, then starts to drop again with great views on the left (west).

23.2   Back at river level. The trail follows the river, then climbs high above.

25.0   Seldom Inn Campground. Continue along the old road.

26.5   Snake Indian Falls. The sign points towards the falls, "200 m": a must stop for anyone on the trail. This waterfall is one of the highlights of the route and one of the most photographed waterfalls in Jasper National Park. After viewing the falls, return to the old road and continue straight ahead.

26.7   Split in the road. The road ahead is blocked by fallen trees. Veer to the left, following the sign. The road turns sharply left towards the river. Turn right onto a single-track trail again following the sign; another sign points ahead to "Horseshoe Meadows in 7.5 km." There are various artefacts along the trail, as well as the remains of an old log fence.

28.5   Junction with the horse trail coming up from the river. Continue on the wide, well-cut, easy-to-travel trail.

31.1   Boardwalk across a marshy area. Continue through the forest, passing the remains of an old log cabin.

33.7   Remains of an old outfitter's camp. The trail continues through the forest and along small meadow-like areas.

34.4   Horseshoe Meadows. This flat, grassy meadow provides great views of the mountains to the west and north.

35.6   Horseshoe Campground. The campground is in a beautiful spot on a bank overlooking the Snake Indian River. Continue along the meadow.

37.2   Trail junction. The trail to Rock Lake and Willow Creek Warden Station goes to the right (north). Continue to the left (west).

37.6   Willow Creek horse camp. This is a large site. Cross Willow Creek on a log bridge and come to Willow Creek Campground in 200 m. The trail continues along a meadow-like area with great views, although the trail is sometimes in the trees.

43.3   Mud Creek junction. The trail to the left (north) goes to Rock

Creek. Continue ahead (west) towards Welbourne Campground. The area continues to be open. Pass through a blow-down area that provides great views all around.

46.7   Deer Creek junction. Glacier Pass and Little Heaven Campground are to the right (northwest). Cross Deer Creek on a bridge and continue ahead (southwest) towards Blue Creek through open meadows and pass a small lake on the right.

49.7   Junction. Welbourne Falls is 400 m to the left (north). Follow along a high bank above the river, pass a campground with a large horse corral, cross Welbourne Creek on a bridge and proceed through the forest.

50.6   Welbourne Campground. Follow the river for a short distance, then enter the forest.

54.0   Bridge over a damp area.

55.3   Milk Creek. The trail remains in the forest with good views straight ahead.

57.4   Nellie Lake. A wide cut trail that looks like a cutline follows through a young pine forest.

61.0   Gate across the trail. The trail follows a high ridge, then drops down towards the river.

61.6   Junction. The trail to the left (south) goes to the Blue Creek Warden Station.

62.5   Blue Creek Campground. From the campground, both the equine and hiking trails go upstream.

62.8   Junction. The trail to the right (north) goes up the east side of Blue Creek to McLaren Pass. Continue along the bank above the creek to another junction, where the horse trail goes left (south) to ford Blue Creek and hikers proceed a short distance to a suspension bridge over the creek.

63.3   Junction. Shortly after returning to the main trail, a heavily-used trail branches right (north) up the Blue Creek valley. Proceed ahead (west), passing a long series of shallow lakes and marshy sections with occasional forays into the forest and near the riverbank. There are good views across the wetlands to glacier-covered mountains.

69.8	Return to the river, passing the remains of an old outfitter's camp. For the most part, the trail follows the river.
74.8	Three Slides Warden Cabin. This is a very open area. The trail follows the river, then climbs a steep bank before returning to the river.
77.5	Three Slides Campground. The trail crosses a large avalanche path, then continues parallel to the river, either in the woods or along the side of a marsh, with the marshes providing great vistas of this wide valley.
80.7	Cross a small stream by rock-hopping. The trail continues to alternate between the forest and marsh with glaciated mountains in full view to the south. As the trail continues west, there are longer stretches along the river.
85.7	Junction. The Hoodoo Warden Cabin is 200 m to the left (south). A sign in the trees points to "Oatmeal Campground, 5 km." The trail runs northwest away from the river, largely in the forest.
88.7	Start climbing towards the pass. The trail returns to the river and follows parallel to the considerably smaller stream.
90.2	Oatmeal Campground. The trail continues uphill with the trees starting to thin out and become smaller. The trail levels out and the scenery becomes very beautiful. The approach to the pass is a broad alpine meadow that gives the appearance of a hay field with scattered trees.
96.5	Snake Indian Pass, indicated by a stake in the ground with a sign on it. Beyond the top of the pass, the terrain remains very open with the rapidly flowing Twintree Creek on the right. The trail becomes rougher and wetter as it drops and enters a narrow treed valley on a high ridge, then drops via switchbacks to creek level.
102.4	Byng Campground and 400 m beyond, Byng Warden Cabin.

The trail continues along a narrow valley through the forest. It is rough and wet in places, with occasional avalanche paths and frequent good views of the surrounding mountains.

107.5 Sign in the trees directing hikers upstream to a bridge. The trail stays largely in the forest, eventually offering a glimpse of Twintree Lake through the trees.

110.7 Lakeshore. The trail follows the lakeshore.

111.9 Twintree Lake Warden Cabin. The trail continues along the lake.

113.6 Twintree Lake Campground. From the end of the lake, the trail begins a long climb through the forest, then drops back to Twintree Creek and an old campsite.

115.8 Twintree Creek bridge. The trail begins a long climb through the forest over a ridge leading to the Smoky River.

118.5 Begin a steep drop with switchbacks. The trail levels out, remaining in heavy forest, then climbs and levels out again.

122.9 Donaldson Creek Campground. The campground has no view and little flat ground. The trail continues downhill through the forest. The forest begins to open up.

125.5 Smoky River Bridge at a very narrow, rocky canyon.

126.0 Junction. There are large painted signs here, one pointing northeast to Jasper via Twintree Lake, another pointing south to the west park boundary via Robson Pass. A Parks Canada sign directs travellers to the lower Smoky River to the right (north) and Chown Creek to the left (south). Take the south trail.

126.4 Smoky River Warden Cabin. Beyond the cabin the trail splits, with the hiking trail going to the right (southwest) through a rocky flood plain with bridges over dry creeks. There are marshes and wetlands on the right (west) and a bridge across Chown Creek.

130.1 Chown Creek Campground. A trail to the right (west) leads up the creek towards Bess Pass. The trail continues to climb through the trees, then down over a ridge before passing a large avalanche path.

133.8	Junction. Timothy Slides horse camp to the left (east). The trail continues parallel to the powerful rushing Smoky River, past avalanche paths which give a good view of the river's gravel flats and the mountain ranges all around.
137.2	Wolverine Warden Cabin. After 500 m, the trail crosses Carcajou Creek on a bridge, continues through the forest, then reaches the Smoky River gravel flats. It continues on a bank just above the gravel flats, with good views all around.
141.2	Wolverine Campground. The trail continues in a very open area along the river, crosses a bridged creek, follows above the river, crosses avalanche paths, then drops down to the gravel flats.
145.9	The approximate end of the gravel flats. The trail rejoins the horse trail and proceeds through the forest. Follow a major stream some distance upstream (west).
147.5	Cross the stream on a bridge, then continue through the forest above the gravel flats of the Smoky River.
151.3	Junction. The trail to Moose Pass goes to the left (northeast). This is km 58.4 of the Fraser River to Moose Pass trail along the Moose River, (trail guide, page 151). The trail to Robson Pass and Berg Lake goes ahead (south). This is km 28.4 of the Fraser River to Robson Pass and the Moose River trail junction along the Robson River (trail guide page 117).

Notes

Introduction

1 Mary L. Jobe Akeley, "A Winter Journey in the Canadian Rockies," *Natural History (The Journal of The American Museum of Natural History)* 32:5 (1932), 508.

2 Arthur Conan Doyle, "The Athabasca Trail," quoted in Peter J. Murphy with Robert W. Udell, Robert E. Stevenson and Thomas W. Peterson, *A Hard Road to Travel: Land, Forests and People in the Upper Athabasca Region* (Hinton, AB: Foothills Model Forest, 2007), 174.

Route I

1 The history of Athabasca Pass and the people who travelled the Athabasca River corridor to reach the pass or return from it is described in detail in Emerson Sanford and Janice Sanford Beck, *Life of the Trail 6: Historic Hikes to Athabasca Pass, Fortress Lake and Tonquin Valley* (Calgary: Rocky Mountain Books, 2011), 33–87.

2 For more information on the Howse Pass route, see Emerson Sanford and Janice Sanford Beck, *Life of the Trail 2: Historic Hikes in Northern Yoho National Park* (Calgary: Rocky Mountain Books, 2008), 24–32.

3 Richard Thomas Wright, *Overlanders: 1858 Gold* (Saskatoon: Western Producer Prairie Books, 1985), 209. When the railway came through the Athabasca River valley at the beginning of the twentieth century, the nose was blasted off Roche Miette, leaving it much as it is today.

4 James G. MacGregor, *Overland by the Yellowhead* (Saskatoon: Western Producer Prairie Books, 1974), 17.

5 Although few details are available, Henry appears to have been the first European to spend a winter in the Jasper area.

6 J.N. Wallace, J.N. Wallace Collection, Bruce Peel Special Collections Library, University of Alberta.

7 MacGregor, preface and 1 and Don Beers, *Jasper-Robson: A Taste of Heaven* (Calgary: Highline Publishing, 1996), 54.

8 Barbara Huck and Doug Whiteway, *In Search of Ancient Alberta* (Winnipeg: Heartland Publications, 1998), 226. A large obsidian point originating from Flow #1 at Anaheim Peak in west-central BC was discovered by a Parks Canada team in 1983 near Jasper on Cabin Creek at the foot of Pyramid Bench. This finding, together with others' findings of projectile points, basalt and petrified wood indicate that people had travelled from the interior of BC east through the Yellowhead Pass for several thousand years and that those people had travel or trade connections in the other direction as well, stretching west almost to the Pacific Coast.

9 *Eastern Slopes Wildlands Our Living Heritage: A Proposal from the Alberta Wilderness Association* (The Alberta Wilderness Association, 1986), 22.

10 MacGregor, 42.

11 Quoted in Peter J. Murphy with Robert W. Udell, Robert E. Stevenson and Thomas W. Peterson, *A Hard Road to Travel: Land, Forests and People in the Upper Athabasca Region* (Hinton, AB: Foothills Model Forest, 2007), 116.

12 Henry John Moberly with William Bleasdell Cameron, *When Fur Was King* (New York: EP Dutton and Co. Inc., 1929), 111.

13 Quoted in Wright, 110.

14 Wright, 130, 142.

15 For information on the southerly routes used by the Overlanders, see Emerson Sanford and Janice Sanford Beck, *Life of the Trail 5: Historic Hikes Around Mount Assiniboine & in Kananaskis Country* (Calgary: Rocky Mountain Books, 2010), 98–100.

16 For more information on James Sinclair's trips, see *Life of the Trail 5*, 30–32 and 92–96.

17 Wright, 214.

18 For information on the Overlanders who used the southern passes, see *Life of the Trail 5*, 98–101.

19 Quoted in Wright, 204.

20 Quoted in Wright, 208.

21 Quoted in Wright, 209.

22 Old Fort Henry (Henry House) was most likely located on the east side of the river.

23 Quoted in Wright, 211.

24 Wright, 212.

25 Ibid.

26 For details of Southesk's trip through the mountains, see Emerson Sanford and Janice Sanford Beck, *Life of the Trail 4: Historic Hikes in Eastern Jasper National Park* (Calgary: Rocky

Mountain Books, 2009), 54–64.

27 Viscount Milton and W.B. Cheadle, *North-West Passage by Land: Being the narrative of an expedition from the Atlantic to the Pacific* (London: Cassell, Petter and Galpin, 1865, reprinted by Coles Publishing Company, Toronto, 1970), 192–96.

28 Ibid,196–97.

29 Ibid, 200.

30 Michael Shaw Bond, *Way out West: On the Trail of an Errant Ancestor* (Toronto: McClelland and Stewart, 2001), 14–26.

31 For details of Southesk's trip through the mountains, see *Life of the Trail 4*, 54–64.

32 Milton and Cheadle, 246–51.

33 Ibid, 254.

34 Ibid, 261.

35 MacGregor, 103.

36 For a brief biography of John Hammond, see *Life of the Trail 2*, 98–100.

37 Muriel Poulton Dunford, *North River: The Story of BC's North Thompson Valley & Yellowhead Highway 5*, Second Edition (Clearwater, BC: Community Resource Centre for the North Thompson, 2008), 70.

38 Ibid, 70–80.

39 For information on the Howse Pass survey, see *Life of the Trail 2*, 37–38.

40 For more information on the Howse Pass route, see *Life of the Trail 2*, 24–32.

41 Daphne Sleigh, *Walter Moberly and the North West Passage by Rail* (Surrey, BC: Hancock House Publishers Ltd., 2003), 189–210.

42 MacGregor, 117.

43 Dunford, 107.

44 MacGregor, 119–20.

45 Dunford, 110.

46 MacGregor, 122.

47 For details of Old Bow Fort, see Emerson Sanford and Janice Sanford Beck, *Life of the Trail 3: The Historic Route from Old Bow Fort to Jasper* (Calgary: Rocky Mountain Books, 2009), 30–33.

48 Hugh A. Dempsey, "A Naturalist at Jasper," *Alberta History* 34:3 (1986), 1–10.

49 MacGregor, 129–30.

50 W.A. Waiser, *The Field Naturalist* (Toronto: University of Toronto Press, 1989), 129.

51 The story of the Coleman brothers' rediscovery of Mount Brown is told in *Life of the Trail 6*, 76–83.

52 The Coleman brothers' trip over Pipestone Pass is described in Emerson Sanford and Janice Sanford Beck, *Life of the Trail 1: Historic Hikes in Eastern Banff National Park* (Calgary: Rocky Mountain Books, 2008), 105–09. Their trip along the Sunwapta and Athabasca rivers to the Miette is detailed in *Life of the Trail 3*, 147–52.

53 A.P. Coleman, *The Canadian Rockies: New & Old Trails* (Calgary: Aquila Books, 1999), 258–59.

54 Ibid, 260.

55 Ibid, 276.

56 Quoted in Donald Phillips, "To the Top of Mount Robson," *Ever Upward: A Century of Canadian Alpine Journals* (*Canadian Alpine Journal* digital edition) 2:2 (1910), 23.

57 A.L. Mumm, "An Expedition to Mount Robson," *Ever Upward: A Century of Canadian Alpine Journals* (*Canadian Alpine Journal* digital edition) 2:2 (1910), 10–20.

58 The youngest member of the group, Ervin Austin MacDonald, detailed their adventures in *The Rainbow Chasers* (Vancouver: Douglas & McIntyre Ltd., 1982).

59 MacDonald, 130.

60 Mary Schäffer's rediscovery of Maligne Lake, approaching from the south, is described in *Life of the Trail 4*, 132–35.

61 The trip along the Sunwapta and Athabasca rivers to Jasper is detailed in *Life of the Trail 3*, 165–66.

62 Mary T.S. Schäffer, *Old Indian Trails of the Canadian Rockies*, forward by Janice Sanford Beck (Calgary: Rocky Mountain Books, 2007), 158–59.

63 Ibid, 161.

64 Ibid, 168.

65 Ibid, 176.

66 Stanley Washburn with Andrew Melrose, *Trails, Trappers and Tenderfeet in Western Canada* (New York and London: Henry Holt and Company, 1912), 125.

67 I.S. MacLaren, *Mapper of Mountains: M.P. Bridgland in the Canadian Rockies 1902–1930* (Edmonton: The University of Alberta Press, 2005), 103.

Route II

1 A.P. Coleman, *The Canadian Rockies: New & Old Trails* (Calgary: Aquila Books, 1999), 264.

2 Frank W. Anderson, "From Wilderness a Park Evolves," *Majestic Jasper Frontier Series No. 30* (Frontier Publishing Ltd, 1973 and Heritage House Publishing Company Ltd., 1980), 10.

3 This trip is described in Route I above, pages 67-68.

4 Coleman, 266.

5 Ibid.

6 Ibid, 267–68.

7 For more details of this climb and its aftermath, see Route III, pages 134–35.

8 Don Beers, *Jasper-Robson: A Taste of Heaven* (Calgary: Highline Publishing, 1996), 184.

9 William C. Taylor, *Tracks Across My Trail: Donald "Curly" Phillips, Guide and Outfitter* (Jasper: Jasper–Yellowhead Historical Society, 1984), 29–30.

10 Esther Fraser, *Wheeler* (Banff: Summerthought, 1978), 102.

11 Kathryn Bridge, *Phyllis Munday: Mountaineer* (Lantzville, BC: XYZ Publishing, 2002), 58–59.

12 A.J. Kaufman and W.L. Putnam, *The Guiding Spirit* (Revelstoke, BC: Footprint Publishing, 1986), 132.

13 Quoted in Cyndi Smith, *Off the Beaten Track: Women Adventurers and Mountaineers in Western Canada* (Lake Louise: Coyote Books, 1989), 108.

14 Mary L. Jobe, "Mount Alexander Mackenzie," *Ever Upward: A Century of Canadian Alpine Journals* (*Canadian Alpine Journal* digital edition) 7 (1916), 62–73.

15 Taylor, 58.

16 Smith, 94.

17 Smith, 109.

18 For more information on Mary Jobe Akeley, see Smith, 80–106.

19 Lillian Gest fonds, Whyte Museum of the Canadian Rockies, M67:41.

20 A.Y. Jackson, *A Painter's Country: The Autobiography of A.Y. Jackson* (Toronto: Clarke, Irwin and Company, 1958), 37.

21 Lisa Christensen, *A Hikers Guide to the Rocky Mountain Art of Lawren Harris* (Calgary: Fifth House, 2000), 18, 20.

22 H.E. Bulyea, "A Trip to Mount Robson," *Ever Upward: A Century of Canadian Alpine Journals* (*Canadian Alpine Journal* digital edition) 10 (1919), 26–31.

23 J. Monroe Thorington, "A Mountaineering Journey Through Jasper Park," *Ever Upward: A Century of Canadian Alpine Journals* (*Canadian Alpine Journal* digital edition) 16 (1926–27), 82.

Route III

1 A.P. Coleman, *The Canadian Rockies: New & Old Trails* (Calgary: Aquila Books, 1999), 303–04.

2 Ibid, 308.

3 Ibid, 314.

4 Chic Scott, "Robson Revisited: Revisiting the controversy over the first ascent of the Monarch of the Rockies," *Mountain Heritage Magazine* 1:2 (Summer 1998), 17.

5 Bruce Fairly, "Defending Mount Robson: The legal considerations of heresay–defending the first ascent of Mt. Robson," *Mountain Heritage Magazine* 3:2 (Summer 2000), 40.

6 J. Norman Collie, "The Canadian Rockies North of Mount Robson," *Appalachia* 12:4 (April 1912), 339–49.

7 Arthur O. Wheeler, "The Alpine Club Of Canada's Expedition To Jasper Park, Yellowhead Pass And Mount Robson Region, 1911," *Ever Upward: A Century of Canadian Alpine Journals* (*Canadian Alpine Journal* digital edition) 4 (1912), 10.

8 Quoted in Ellis L. Yochelson, *Smithsonian Institution Secretary: Charles Doolittle Walcott* (Ohio: Kent State University Press, 2001), 106.

9 Ibid.

10 James G. MacGregor, *Vision of an Ordered Land: The Story of the Dominion Land Survey* (Saskatoon: Western Producer Prairie Books, 1981), 162.

11 Donald Phillips, "Winter Conditions North and West of Mt. Robson," *Ever Upward: A Century of Canadian Alpine Journals* (*Canadian Alpine Journal* digital edition) 6 (1914–15), 128.

12 Lawrence J. Burpee, *Among the Canadian Alps* (Toronto: Bell and Cockburn, 1914), 215. Burpee helped found the Canadian Historical Association and was the founding editor of the *Canadian Geographical Journal*.

13 Ibid, 216–17.

14 Ibid, 220.

15 Ibid, 201.

16 Cyndi Smith, *Off the Beaten Track: Women Adventurers and Mountaineers in Western Canada* (Lake Louise: Coyote Books, 1989), 88.

17 Lillian Gest fonds, Whyte Museum of the Canadian Rockies, M67:41.

18 For information on Caroline Hinman's trip into the Tonquin Valley, see Emerson Sanford and Janice Sanford Beck, *Life of the Trail 6: Historic Hikes to Athabasca Pass, Fortress Lake and Tonquin Valley* (Calgary: Rocky Mountain Books, 2010), 146.

19 For a brief biography of A.Y. Jackson, see *Life of the Trail 6*, 141–44.

20 Lisa Christensen, *Guide to the Rocky Mountain Art of Lawren Harris* (Calgary: Fifth House, 2000), 29.

21 For a brief biography of Lawren Harris, see Emerson Sanford and Janice Sanford Beck, *Life of the Trail 4:Historic Hikes in Eastern Jasper National Park* (Calgary: Rocky Mountain Books, 2009), 166–67.

22 Christensen, 42.

23 For a brief biography of Carl Rungius, see *Life of the Trail 4*, 128–29.

24 Quoted in Jon Whyte and E.J. Hart, *Painter of the Western Wilderness* (Vancouver and Toronto: The Glenbow–Alberta Institute in association with Douglas McIntyre, 1985), 118.

Route IV

1 Barbara Huck and Doug Whiteway, *In Search of Ancient Alberta* (Winnipeg: Heartland Publications, 1998), 236.

2 Don Beers, *Jasper–Robson: A Taste of Heaven* (Calgary: Highline Publishing, 1996), 72.

3 For more information on Jacques Cardinal, see Emerson Sanford and Janice Sanford Beck, *Life of the Trail 4:Historic Hikes in Eastern Jasper National Park* (Calgary: Rocky Mountain Books, 2009), 52.

4 James G. MacGregor, *Overland by the Yellowhead* (Saskatoon: Western Producer Prairie Books, 1974), 45–46.

5 Quoted in E.J. Hart, *Diamond Hitch: The Early Outfitters and Guides of Banff and Jasper* (Banff: Summerthought, 1979), 100.

6 William C. Taylor, *The Snows of Yesteryear: J. Norman Collie, Mountaineer* (Toronto: Holt, Rinehart and Winston, 1973), 151.

7 Samuel Prescott Fay, *The Forgotten Explorer: Samuel Prescott Fay's 1914 Expedition to the Northern Rockies*, edited by Charles Helm and Mike Murtha, forward by Robert William Sandford (Surrey BC: Rocky Mountain Books, 2009), 234.

8 Fay named the peak Mount Alexander, a name which was later changed to Mount Sir Alexander to honour an earlier explorer, Sir Alexander Mackenzie.

9 Fay, 234–35.

10 Ibid, 6.

11 Ibid, 11.

12 Caroline B. Hinman, "A Pack Train Trip, North From Jasper, Alberta," *Ever Upward: A Century of Canadian Alpine Journals* (*Canadian Alpine Journal* digital edition) 13 (1923), 146–52.

13 A.S. Sibbald, "North of Mount Robson," *Ever Upward: A Century of Canadian Alpine Journals* (*Canadian Alpine Journal* digital edition) 16 (1926–27), 147–53. Sibbald was a pioneer in mountain travel without horses [see Emerson Sanford and Janice Sanford Beck, *Life of the Trail 5: Historic Hikes around Mount Assiniboine & in Kananaskis Country* (Calgary: Rocky Mountain Books, 2010), 199–202] and although backpacks during the 1920s were primitive and lightweight camping equipment was still in the future, their trip was a harbinger of things to come.

14 A.J. Gilmore, "Beyond Mount Robson: First Ascent of Mount Sir Alexander," *Ever Upward: A Century of Canadian Alpine Journals* (*Canadian Alpine Journal* digital edition) 18 (1929), 22-33.

IMAGE CREDITS

Page 30 All nineteenth-century travellers proceeding through the Athabasca River valley faced the unenviable choice of either fording the Athabasca River or climbing the difficult trail over Disaster Point. This 1863 sketch by Dr. Cheadle shows Louis Battenotte (The Assiniboine) leading a pack horse with the artist urging it to climb the steep trail from behind. (Glenbow Museum and Archives, NA 1240-8)

Page 32 *The Parting of the Brigades 1826* by Walter J. Phillips illustrates the Yellowhead Pass group of the westbound Hudson's Bay Company brigade continuing west along the Miette (with Pyramid Mountain in the background) and the Athabasca Pass group fording the Miette River en route to the Whirlpool. (Hudson's Bay Company Archives, Archives of Manitoba, P-402)

Page 35 Most of the Overlanders were men from eastern Canada and the United States seeking wealth and fame in the gold fields of the Cariboo. Thomas McMicking, leader of one of the largest parties to cross the continent, was known for his exceptional efficiency and integrity. (Royal British Columbia Museum, British Columbia Archives, A-01418)

Page 36 Francis Augustus Schubert was a member of the large McMicking party of Overlanders that crossed Yellowhead Pass en route to Tête Jaune Cache and the gold fields of the Cariboo. He was exceptional only in that his wife and three children accompanied him on this ambitious journey. (Royal British Columbia Museum, British Columbia Archives, A-03080)

Page 37 Catherine Schubert crossed the continent with her husband and three children as part of the McMicking party of Overlanders. Unknown to the group, she was pregnant at the time and soon after they arrived at Fort Kamloops gave birth to the first white child in central British Columbia. Though Métis women often travelled while pregnant and gave birth on the trail, it was unusual for a white woman to do so. (Royal British Columbia Museum, British Columbia Archives, A-03081)

Page 41 Tête Jaune Cache was located at a natural crossroads – the head of navigation for the Fraser River – and played a major role in the construction of the Canadian Northern and Grand Trunk Pacific railroads early in the twentieth century. This 1911 image shows it as a booming frontier town, very different from the 1860s when it was little more than a name with a few shacks. The original site is now submerged by the Fraser River. (Jasper-Yellowhead Museum and Archives, PA-49-5)

Page 45 Mr. O'Beirne, the ne'er do well parasite who attached himself to the Milton and Cheadle party to cross the mountains in 1863, was deathly afraid of mounting a horse – even in order to cross deep rushing rivers. This sketch by Dr. Cheadle shows how he used the tail of Cheadle's horse Bucephalus to maintain his balance on the treacherous crossing. (Glenbow Museum and Archives, NA 1240-13)

Page 48 One of the most unlikely groups to cross the mountains from Fort Edmonton to Fort Victoria in the mid 1800s was made up of Viscount Lord Milton and his personal physician and friend, Dr. Walter Cheadle. The pair, guided by Louis Battonette (The Assiniboine) was exploring the country with no specific objective. The entire party, shown here, consisted of: (l–r) Mrs. Battenotte, Louis Battenotte (The Assiniboine), Dr. Walter Cheadle, Viscount Lord Milton, and the Battonette's son Baptiste. (Royal British Columbia Museum, British Columbia Archives, A-00601)

Page 51 Viscount Lord Milton was the eldest son of the 6th Earl of Fitzwilliam and as such, was in line to inherit his father's title and massive fortune. Lord Milton was epileptic, however, a condition which was not accepted by the upper-class Britons of the time. Milton's trip across Canada was likely predicated on a desire to escape the societal stigma he faced. (Royal British Columbia Museum, British Columbia Archives, A-02651)

Page 56 This sketch by Dr. Cheadle illustrates one of many instances when Louis Battenotte (The Assiniboine) made a heroic effort to save the party from grief. He plunged into the dangerous rapid to grab the horse and help it to safety. The other horse in the sketch, together with the pack containing valuable necessities, was irretrievably lost. (Glenbow Museum and Archives, NA 1240-11)

Page 57 Dr. John Rae, a Hudson's Bay Company doctor, established a reputation for efficient northern travel during his Arctic search for the lost Franklin expedition. As a result, he was chosen to locate a possible wagon road and telegraph line to connect the West Coast with central Canada. (Glenbow Museum and Archives, NA 1252-2)

Page 59 When the federal government decided to build a railroad to connect the new province of British Columbia to the eastern provinces, Yellowhead Pass was initially the favoured route.

This image shows Chief Dominion Geologist Alfred Selwyn seated at centre, with artist and photographer John Hammond on his right and photographer Benjamin Baltzy on his left, together with five unidentified assistants, during a 1871 geological survey from the coast to Yellowhead Pass. (Library and Archives Canada, FA-057)

Page 60 Sandford Fleming was named chief surveyor in charge of finding the best route through the mountains for the proposed transcontinental railway. In 1872 he travelled across Canada to have a first-hand look at his favoured route, the gentle Yellowhead Pass. The group here, decked out in the travelling garb of the era is (l-r) Frank Fleming, Sandford Fleming, Dr. Grant and Dr. Arthur Moren. (Library and Archives Canada, FA-057 (1872))

Page 61 Although Walter Moberly was one of Fleming's surveyors, he had his heart set on Howse Pass as a route for the railway. The men's difference of opinion led to a historic 1872 meeting between the two in Jasper. A local Métis created a Lobstick tree along the river in Jasper to commemorate the meeting, known locally as the Moberly Lobstick tree. Lobstick trees are created by trimming all the lower branches of a tree to create a landmark with which to honour someone. Although created in 1872, this Lobstick tree was still in good health more than 60 years later, as shown in this 1935 image. In 2004 the tree was still standing as a decaying snag. (Jasper-Yellowhead Museum and Archives, PA 18-54)

Page 63 The Henderson family (1884). Thomas and Percy (standing, back row), and Walter, Margaret (Peggy), Margaret, Charles, Olive, Janet and Agnes (front row, l-r), migrated from New Westminster, British Columbia to Edmonton, Alberta in 1880 to take up land before the railway arrived. Although the railway was re-routed to the south, the family nonetheless established a successful farming operation south of Edmonton. (City of Edmonton Archives, EA-80-2)

Page 64 This 1898 photo shows the innovative Henderson barn on the family's Rabbit Hill farm. Charles Henderson is on the left with his wife and baby Ella third from the left. The lady on the right is listed as Mrs. Henderson's mother, holding the hand of young Bill Sutherland. Second from the left is Mrs. Mike Ryan and child Stanley Ryan. The barn is now located at Fort Edmonton Park. (The lines are scratches on the old photo.) (City of Edmonton Archives, EA-80-4)

Page 65 In 1895, Lewis Swift brought his bride, Suzette Chalifoux, to the log house he had built in the Athabasca valley near present-day Jasper. They welcomed everyone who travelled through the valley and often treated them to freshly grown produce from the garden and milk and eggs from the farm. This image, taken in 1908, shows Suzette and four of her children near the family home, "Swift's Place". (Whyte Museum of the Canadian Rockies, V527 PS-94)

Page 73 Early in the twentieth century, Mary Schäffer, a Philadelphia Quaker who later moved to Banff, set two precedents in Rocky Mountain travel. Not only was she the first non-indigenous woman to explore extensively in the Rocky Mountains, but some considered her means of doing so – going into the wilderness for extended periods with a female companion and two unrelated men – to be scandalous. Today she is considered a pioneer and hero. She is seen here on her favourite horse, Nibs. (Whyte Museum of the Canadian Rockies, V14 AC 55 PD-18)

Page 76 Fred Stephens, who made his home base east of the mountains in Lacombe, Alberta, was one of the early Rocky Mountain outfitters. One of his repeat customers was Stanley Washburn, who had a burning desire to reach Tête Jaune Cache. After several attempts he finally fulfilled his dream. Stephens is seen here sitting on a makeshift backcountry table that he and his helpers likely built. (Glenbow Museum and Archives, NA 3551-7)

Page 77 Sir Arthur Conan Doyle, creator of Sherlock Holmes and one of the most popular writers of his time, was persuaded to visit Jasper in 1914. This image of a family picnic was taken on his second visit in 1923. Back row, l-r, unidentified, Arthur Conan Doyle (reclining), packers Ray Scott and Bob LeStrang and guide Closson Otto (with hat). In front are the three Conan Doyle children, Adrian, Jean and Dennis and their mother, Lady Jean Conan Doyle. (Jasper-Yellowhead Museum and Archives, PA33-31)

Page 93 Reverend George Kinney was a man of God who preferred to work with underprivileged people in small isolated communities. As a young man, he became obsessed with being the first person to climb Mount Robson. His efforts on that mountain are still regarded as one of the outstanding achievements of Canadian mountaineering history. (Royal British Columbia Museum, British Columbia Archives, E-00042)

Page 97 This 1909 British party consisting of (l-r, back row) climbers A.L. Mumm and L.S. Amery with Swiss guide Moritz Inderbinen, outfitter John Yates, two unidentified packers, [sitting, (l-r)] another unidentified packer, climber Geoffrey Hastings, packer James Shand-Harvey and a fourth unidentified packer were heading towards Mount Robson intent on climbing the mountain when George Kinney informed them that he had already done so. (Whyte Museum of the Canadian Rockies, V64 PD-1)

Page 98 In 1911 Alpine Club of Canada (ACC) president Arthur Wheeler organized an expedition of Smithsonian scientists and ACC members to explore the Mount Robson area. Part of Wheeler's objective was to determine if an ACC camp could be held in the area. The portion of the group shown here consists of (l-r) President Wheeler, outfitter Curly Phillips, scientists Harry Blagden, J.H. Riley, and Charles Walcott, Jr., with packers James Shand-Harvey and Casey Jones standing and ACC helper Reverend George Kinney seated. (Whyte Museum of the Canadian Rockies, V 263 NA-5999)

Page 99 The Moose Pass route was too long and difficult to provide adequate access to the Alpine Club of Canada climbing camp at Mount Robson. Curly Phillips was given the task of building an alternate trail up the Robson River. The flying trestle bridge seen here under construction in 1913 was part of this new trail. The bridge lasted well into the twentieth century, but was eventually replaced with a series of switchbacks on a re-routed trail. (Jasper-Yellowhead Museum and Archives, 991.96.02.02.04)

Page 101 The husband and wife team of Don and Phyl Munday, seen here on the top of Mount Victoria, near Lake Louise, were accomplished climbers who climbed mainly on the West Coast of British Columbia. Phyl had her heart set on climbing Mount Robson; her dream came true at the Alpine Club of Canada's 1924 camp, making her the first woman to summit the peak. (Royal British Columbia Museum, British Columbia Archives, I-51588)

Page 102 This 1915 image shows Caroline Hinman on the left with Mary Jobe and outfitter Curly Phillips. The three met at the 1913 Alpine Club of Canada camp and completed a major pack-train trip in 1915. A romance developed between Phillips and Jobe, who travelled together several times. (Jasper-Yellowhead Museum and Archives, PA-38-23)

Page 107 Curly Phillips and Mary Jobe with Phillips' dog, likely taken on their 1915 trip north of Mount Robson. Jobe's fall 1917 trip with Phillips was her final visit to the Canadian Rockies. (Jasper-Yellowhead Museum and Archives, 991.91.14.04)

Page 110 Caroline Hinman, who became famous for escorting American teenage girls through the mountains on her Off the Beaten Track tours, spent many summers touring in the Canadian Rockies. (Whyte Museum of the Canadian Rockies, V225 PD-7-49)

Page 127 Adolphus Moberly, an Iroquois Métis who lived in the Jasper area, was known to be a tireless worker of powerful physique and very knowledgeable about the area around Yellowhead Pass and Mount Robson. He led outfitter John Yates up the Moose River on the trail that approaches Mount Robson from the east. (Whyte Museum of the Canadian Rockies, F 1090 C-6)

Page 131 In 1897 Lewis Swift brought his bride, Suzette Chalifoux, to the area east of Jasper. For many years the family home was a landmark in the Athabasca valley, welcoming all who passed through. This image was taken in 1928, in front of their log home. (Jasper-Yellowhead Museum and Archives, 997.07.314.05 (1928))

Page 132 Lewis Swift was a creative pioneer who built this water wheel to power the grist mill he used to grind grain. This image was taken in 1909 when a survey crew was working in the area. Another of his innovations was to use cut sections from a large Douglas fir tree as wagon wheels. (Jasper-Yellowhead Museum and Archives, PA 44-23)

Page 137 Arthur Wheeler, president of the Alpine Club of Canada (ACC), wanted both to assess the feasibility of holding an ACC climbing camp at Robson Pass and to do a scientific investigation of the area. The Canadian contingent consisted of (l-r) packer James Shand-Harvey, climber Reverend George Kinney, Swiss guide Conrad Kain and outfitter Curly Phillips with President Wheeler on the far right. The Smithsonian Institution scientists seated between Phillips and Wheeler are (l-r) Charles Walcott Jr., Harry Blagden, Ned Hollister and J.H. Riley. (Whyte Museum of the Canadian Rockies, V263 NA-1148)

Page 138 Charles Walcott was accompanied by family members, friends and Smithsonian Institution (SI) scientists on his second trip to Mount Robson. He took this photo of (l-r)

Sydney Walcott, Dr. I.F. Burgen (SI), Walcott's camp manager Arthur Brown, Harry Blagden (SI), R.C.W. Lett of the Grand Trunk Pacific Railway and outfitter Clossen Otto. (Jasper-Yellowhead Museum and Archives, 991.96.02.03.02)

Page 144 Lawren Harris, a membeer of the Group of Seven artists, made many trips to the Rockies to paint. His destinations include Mount Robson, Tonquin Valley, Maligne Lake and Lake O'Hara. He is seen here in 1946 standing in front of a painting by now-famous West Coast artist Emily Carr. (Royal British Columbia Museum, British Columbia Archives, I-51570)

Page 145 Carl Rungius began painting in the Canadian Rockies when outfitter Jimmy Simpson invited him to accompany him on a backcountry trip in 1910. He subsequently travelled and painted widely in the Rockies and eventually moved to Banff. (Glenbow Museum and Archives, NA 633-9 (1925))

Page 159 During the first half of the nineteenth century, Britain's large botanical centres were sending botanists worldwide to collect plant specimens for their permanent collections. Thomas Drummond, the first to collect in the Jasper area, travelled widely over territory that had never before seen an European. Later explorers along the Snake Indian River seemed to be unaware of Drummond's travels. (Royal Botanic Gardens, Kew Library and Archives, Slide R8G Kew)

Page 161 John Yates was an outfitter who worked out of the Lac St. Anne area west of Edmonton. He led several trips up the Moose River to Berg Lake and seemed to have a sixth sense for route-finding in unknown country. He led the first well-recorded trip from the base of Mount Robson to the Athabasca River, using his uncanny abilities to turn up a side valley that led to Snake Indian Pass. (Whyte Museum of the Canadian Rockies, NA 33-1709)

Page 166 Samuel Prescott Fay made Rocky Mountain history with his 1914 five-month wilderness expedition from Jasper north to Hudson's Hope on the Peace River. His exact route has never been duplicated in one continuous trip. Fortunately for lovers of wilderness travel, Fay kept a detailed diary which has recently been published. (Jasper-Yellowhead Museum and Archives, 84.87.250)

Page 172 The Fay group towards the end of their epic five-month wilderness trek. This image was taken at the Hudson's Bay Co. trading post on the Peace River. The group (l–r): Charles Prescott Fay, his friend Charles Cross, helpers Bob Jones and Jack Symes and outfitter Fred Brewster, are looking remarkably fit and hardy after such a long, and at times trying, trip. (Jasper-Yellowhead Museum and Archives, 84.87.251)

Page 174 Fred Brewster, a member of Banff's prominent Brewster family, moved north and settled in Jasper in 1912. He mostly worked as an outfitter during his early years in Jasper but gradually expanded his business interests to become an influential and well-loved businessman. He was known by most simply as Major Brewster, a title earned during his war service. (Jasper-Yellowhead Museum and Archives, PA-34-6)

Page 179 Andrew Sibbald's chance encounter with Hebert Sampson (l) in Saskatoon in 1916 set Sibbald's life on a new path. It was Sampson who introduced Sibbald to mountaineering. Always interested in trying new things, the pair hiked without horses through untracked country from Jackpine Pass back to Robson Station. (Courtesy Betty Anne Muckle)

All other photographs: Emerson Sanford, unless otherwise noted

BIBLIOGRAPHY

Akeley, Mary L. Jobe. "A Winter Journey in the Canadian Rockies." *Natural History (The Journal of The American Museum of Natural History)* 32:5 (1932): 508-20.

Anderson, Frank W. "From Wilderness a Park Evolves," *Majestic Jasper Frontier Series No. 30.* Frontier Publishing Ltd, 1973 and Heritage House Publishing Company Ltd., 1980: 4-35.

Eastern Slopes Wildlands Our Living Heritage: A Proposal from The Alberta Wilderness Association. The Alberta Wilderness Association, 1986.

Beers, Don. *Jasper-Robson: A Taste of Heaven: Scenes, Tales, Trails.* Calgary: Highline Publishing, 1996.

Bond, Michael Shaw. *Way out West: On the Trail of an Errant Ancestor.* Toronto: McClelland and Stewart, 2001.

Bridge, Kathryn. *Phyllis Munday, Mountaineer.* Lantzville, BC: XYZ Publishing, 2002.

Bulyea, H.E. "A Trip to Mount Robson." *Ever Upward: A Century of Canadian Alpine Journals (Canadian Alpine Journal* digital edition) 10 (1919): 26-31.

Burpee, Lawrence J. *Among the Canadian Alps.* Toronto: Bell and Cockburn, 1914.

Christensen, Lisa. *A Hikers Guide to the Rocky Mountain Art of Lawren Harris.* Calgary: Fifth House Ltd., 2000.

Coleman, A.P. *The Canadian Rockies: New & Old Trails.* Calgary: Aquila Books, 1999.

Collie, J. Norman. "The Canadian Rockies North of Mount Robson." *Appalachia* 12:4 (April 1912): 339-49.

Dempsey, Hugh A. "A Naturalist at Jasper." *Alberta History* 34:3 (1986): 1-10.

Dunford, Muriel Poulton. *North River: The Story of BC's North Thompson Valley & Yellowhead Highway 5,* second edition. Clearwater, BC: Community Resource Centre for the North Thompson, 2008.

Fairly, Bruce. "Defending Mount Robson: The legal considerations of heresay—defending the first ascent of Mt. Robson." *Mountain Heritage Magazine* 3:2 (Summer 2000): 34-40.

Fay, Samuel Prescott. *The Forgotten Explorer: Samuel Prescott Fay's 1914 Expedition to the Northern Rockies,* edited by Charles Helm and Mike Murtha, forward by Robert William Sandford. Surrey BC: Rocky Mountain Books, 2009.

Fraser, Esther. *Wheeler.* Banff: Summerthought Ltd., 1978.

Gilmore, A.J. "Beyond Mount Robson: First Ascent of Mount Sir Alexander." *Ever Upward: A Century of Canadian Alpine Journals (Canadian Alpine Journal* digital edition) 18 (1929): 22-33.

Grant, Reverend George M. *Ocean to Ocean: Sandford Fleming's Expedition through Canada in 1872.* Rutland, Vermont: Charles E. Tuttle, 1967.

Hart, E. J. *Diamond Hitch: The Early Outfitters and Guides of Banff and Jasper.* Banff: Summerthought Ltd., 1979.

Hart, E. J., ed. *A Hunter of Peace, Mary Schaffer's Old Indian Trails of the Canadian Rockies.* Banff: The Whyte Foundation, 1980.

Hinman, Caroline B. "A Pack Train Trip, North From Jasper, Alberta." *Ever Upward: A Century of Canadian Alpine Journals (Canadian Alpine Journal* digital edition) 13 (1923): 146-52.

Hubbard, Mina Benson. *The Woman who Mapped Labrador: The Life and Expedition Diary of Mina Hubbard,* with diary introduced and edited by Roberta Buchanan and Bryan Greene and biography by Anne Hart. Montreal and Kingston: McGill-Queen's University Press, 2005.

Huck, Barbara and Doug Whiteway. *In Search of Ancient Alberta.* Winnipeg: Heartland Publications, 1998.

J.N. Wallace Collection. Bruce Peel Special Collections Library. Edmonton: University of Alberta.

Jackson, A.Y. *A Painter's Country: The Autobiography of A Y. Jackson.* Toronto: Clarke, Irwin and Company, 1958.

Jobe, Mary L. "Mount Alexander Mackenzie." *Ever Upward: A Century of Canadian Alpine Journals* (*Canadian Alpine Journal* digital edition) 7 (1916): 62-73.

Kain, Conrad. *Where the Clouds Can Go*, original forewords by J. Monroe Thorington & Hans Gmoser, new foreword by Pat Morrow, edited with additional chapters by J. Monroe Thorington. Calgary: Rocky Mountain Books, 2009.

Kaufman, A.J. and W.L. Putnam. *The Guiding Spirit*. Revelstoke, BC: Footprint Publishing, 1986.

Lillian Gest fonds. Whyte Museum of the Canadian Rockies. Banff, Alberta. M67:41.

MacDonald, Irvin Austin. *The Rainbow Chasers*. Vancouver: Douglas & McIntyre, 1982.

MacGregor, James G. *Overland by the Yellowhead*. Saskatoon: Western Producer Prairie Books, 1974.

MacGregor, James G. *Vision of an Ordered Land: The Story of the Dominion Land Survey*. Saskatoon: Western Producer Prairie Books, 1981.

MacLaren, I.S. *Mapper of Mountains: M.P. Bridgland in the Canadian Rockies 1902 - 1930*. Edmonton: The University of Alberta Press, 2005.

Milton, Viscount and W.B. Cheadle. *North-West Passage by Land: being the narrative of an expedition from the Atlantic to the Pacific*. London: Cassell, Petter and Galpin, 1865, reprinted by Coles Publishing Company, Toronto, 1970.

Moberly, Henry John, with William Bleasdell Cameron. *When Fur Was King*. New York: EP Dutton, 1929.

Mumm, A.L. "An Expedition to Mount Robson." *Ever Upward: A Century of Canadian Alpine Journals* (*Canadian Alpine Journal* digital edition) 2 (1910): 10-20.

Murphy, Peter J., with Robert W. Udell, Robert E. Stevenson and Thomas W. Peterson. *A Hard Road to Travel: Land, Forests and People in the Upper Athabasca Region*. Hinton, AB: Foothills Model Forest, 2007.

Phillips, Donald. "To the Top of Mount Robson," *Ever Upward: A Century of Canadian Alpine Journals* (*Canadian Alpine Journal* digital edition) 2 (1910): 21-32.

Phillips, Donald. "Winter Conditions North and West of Mt. Robson." *Ever Upward: A Century of Canadian Alpine Journals* (*Canadian Alpine Journal* digital edition) 6 (1914–15): 128-35.

Sanford, Emerson and Janice Sanford Beck. *Life of the Trail 1: Historic Hikes in Eastern Banff National Park*. Calgary: Rocky Mountain Books, 2008.

Sanford, Emerson and Janice Sanford Beck. *Life of the Trail 2: Historic Hikes in Northern Yoho National Park*. Calgary: Rocky Mountain Books, 2008.

Sanford, Emerson and Janice Sanford Beck. *Life of the Trail 3: The Historic Route from Old Bow Fort to Jasper*. Calgary: Rocky Mountain Books, 2009.

Sanford, Emerson and Janice Sanford Beck. *Life of the Trail 4: Historic Hikes in Eastern Jasper National Park*. Calgary: Rocky Mountain Books, 2009.

Sanford, Emerson and Janice Sanford Beck. *Life of the Trail 5: Historic Hikes Around Mount Assiniboine & in Kananaskis Country*. Calgary: Rocky Mountain Books, 2010.

Sanford, Emerson and Janice Sanford Beck. *Life of the Trail 6: Historic Hikes to Athabasca Pass, Fortress Lake and Tonquin Valley*. Calgary: Rocky Mountain Books, 2011.

Schäffer, Mary T.S. *Old Indian Trails of the Canadian Rockies*, with a forward by Janice Sanford Beck. Calgary: Rocky Mountain Books, 2007.

Scott, Chic. "Robson Revisited: Revisiting the controversy over the first ascent of the Monarch of the Rockies." *Mountain Heritage Magazine* 1:2 (Summer 1998): 14-17.

Sibbald, A.S. "North of Mount Robson." *Ever Upward: A Century of Canadian Alpine Journals* (*Canadian Alpine Journal* digital edition) 17 (1926–27): 147-53.

Sleigh, Daphne. *Walter Moberly and the North West Passage by Rail*. Surrey, BC: Hancock House, 2003.

Smith, Cyndi. *Off the Beaten Track: Women Adventurers and Mountaineers in Western Canada*. Lake Louise: Coyote Books, 1989.

Taylor, William C. *The Snows of Yesteryear: J. Norman Collie, Mountaineer*. Toronto: Holt, Rinehart and Winston of Canada, Limited, 1973.

Taylor, William C. *Tracks across My Trail: Donald "Curly" Phillips, Guide and Outfitter*. Jasper: Jasper–Yellowhead Historical Society, 1984.

Thorington, J. Monroe. "A Mountaineering Journey Through Jasper Park." *Ever Upward: A Century of Canadian Alpine Journals* (*Canadian Alpine Journal* digital edition) 16 (1926–27): 71-85.

Waiser, W.A. *The Field Naturalist*. Toronto: University of Toronto Press, 1989.

Washburn, Stanley W., with Andrew Melrose. *Trails, Trappers and Tenderfeet in Western Canada*. New York and London: Henry Holt and Company, 1912.

Wheeler, Arthur O. "The Alpine Club Of Canada's Expedition To Jasper Park, Yellowhead Pass And Mount Robson Region, 1911." *Ever Upward: A Century of Canadian Alpine Journals* (*Canadian Alpine Journal* digital edition) 4 (1912): 8-80.

Whyte, Jon and E.J. Hart. *Painter of the Western Wilderness*. Vancouver and Toronto: The Glenbow-Alberta Institute in association with Douglas McIntyre, 1985.

Wright, Richard Thomas. *Overlanders: 1858 Gold*. Saskatoon: Western Producer Prairie Books, 1985.

Yochelson, Ellis L. *Smithsonian Institution Secretary: Charles Doolittle Walcott*. Ohio: The Kent State University Press, 2001.

INDEX

About the Authors

Image courtesy of Shawn Sanford Beck

Emerson Sanford, originally from Nova Scotia, first visited the mountains of western Canada in the summer of 1961. Eleven years later, he moved to Alberta and has been hiking ever since. After beginning to backpack seriously with his teenaged daughters in 1990, he began to wonder who cut the trails and how their routing had been determined, Since then, not only has he delved through printed material about the trails, he has also solo hiked every historic route and most long trails between Mount Robson and the Kananaskis Lakes – over 3000 kilometers over five years! Emerson now lives in Canmore with his wife, Cheryl.

Janice Sanford Beck is the author of the best-selling No Ordinary Woman: The Story of Mary Schäffer Warren (Rocky Mountain Books, 2001). She has also written the introduction to the latest edition of Mary T.S. Schäffer's Old Indian Trails of the Canadian Rockies (Rocky Mountain Books 2007) and, with Cheryl Sanford, researched the Mary Schäffer Warren portion of the Glenbow Museum's new permanent exhibit, Mavericks. Janice is presently masquerading as a flatlander, making her home in Saskatoon with her partner, Shawn, and their three children.

Every Trail Has A Story

ISBN 978-1-897522-41-7   RMBooks

... and the stories of early travel along what are today's Highway 1A, the Trans-Canada Highway and the Icefields Parkway are detailed in this volume. The starting point, Old Bow Fort, located on the west end of the Morley reserve, is the remains of the old fur trading fort, Peigan Post. Before roads were built, a horse trail led along the Bow River from Old Bow Fort to today's Lake Louise. Travels along this route form Route I of this volume.

Prior to the 1930s, the horse trail leading north from Lake Louise to the Columbia Icefields was the busiest route in the Rockies as tourists sought new adventures and mountaineers attempted to reach the base of challenging mountains. This section of the Icefields Parkway is described in Route II.

In 1896, Walter Wilcox discovered today's Wilcox Pass which pack trains subsequently used to circumvent the Columbia Icefields. The outfitters could continue north to the Athabasca River. Stories of those who advanced north are given in Route III.

Each volume contains current and historical images of people and places along the route and biographies of important historical figures.

These books are available from Emerson Sanford at emsanf@telus.net for $22.95 each, including shipping to Canadian addresses at no additional charge.

Every Trail

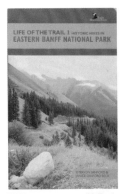

ISBN 978-1-894765-99-2 RMBooks

ISBN 9781-897522-00-4 RMBooks

ISBN 978-1-897522-80-6 RMBooks

... and the stories of the historic trails in the area south of the North Saskatchewan River – Columbia Icefields are detailed in these three volumes and the forthcoming *Life of the Trail 8 Historic Hikes around Lakes Louise and O'Hara and the Rockwall* (Spring 2013). The four volumes cover historic trails in Banff, Yoho and Kootenay National Parks as well as Mount Assiniboine and Height of the Rockies Provincial Parks, Kananaskis Country and the Siffleur and Bighorn Wildnerness Areas.

The stories start with David Thompson, the first European to record entering the Rocky Mountains, and his early adventures travelling along the Red Deer River and subsequently over Howse Pass. Later, mountaineers used Pipestone Pass to access the North Saskatchewan River and Howse Pass and developed a new route back to Field over Amiskwi Pass. Walter Wilcox and Bill Peyto first explored the Sawback Range and Caroline Hinman was the first to follow today's Cascade Fire Road north to the Red Deer River, continuing over Divide Summit and Whiterabbit Pass to the North Saskatchewan River.

World famous mountaineer Edward Whymper cut trails into the Yoho Valley and the Castleguard Meadows were explored by Charles Walcott of Burgess Shale fame. White Man and North Kananaskis passes were first utilized in the fur trade era whereas it was twentieth century explorers who found routes to the Mount Assiniboine area. Bill Peyto sought refuge in the Egypt Lakes area and established a talc mine there. Early explorations in the Lakes Louise and O'Hara areas and the Rockwall will be contained in the forthcoming *Life of the Trail 8*.

Each volume contains a complete up-to-date trail guide for the routes discussed, as well as current and historical images and biographies of important figures.

These books are available from Emerson Sanford at emsanf@telus.net for $22.95 each, including shipping to Canadian addresses at no additional charge.

Has A Story

... and the stories of historic trails in Jasper National Park and the adjoining areas of Mount Robson Provincial Park and the Whitegoat Wilderness are told in these three volumes. The amazing fur trade routes of Michael Klyne along the Maligne River and Poboktan Creek and of Jacques Cardinal along the Rocky and Medicine Tent rivers, Job and Coral creeks, between the Athabasca and North Saskatchewan rivers are described. The Coleman brothers, with the help of their Native guide, later discovered the Cline River–Cataract Creek–Jonas Pass route to the Sunwapta River. Early in the twentieth century, Fred Brewster laid out the very popular Skyline Trail.

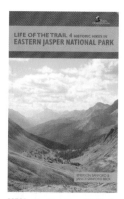

ISBN 978-1-897522-42-4 RMBooks

David Thompson established the Athabasca Pass route over the Rockies in 1911 which served as part of the trans-continental fur trade route for nearly 50 years. The Coleman brothers accidently discovered Fortress Lake while searching for the supposed giants, Mounts Brown and Hooker, near Athabasca Pass. The now popular Tonquin Valley was first entered by surveyor M.P. Bridgland early in the twentieth century.

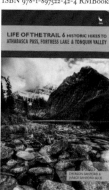

Trials experienced by the Overlanders in crossing Yellowhead Pass en route to Tête Jaune Cache were also experienced by the tourists Milton and Cheadle who used the same route. The Coleman brothers utilized the pass in early attempts to reach and climb Mount Robson by travelling along the Robson River. They successfully reached the base of the mountain by following a route along the Moose River and crossing Moose Pass, thanks to Métis guide Adolphus Moberly. The Robson River route became a reality after Curly Phillips and Frank Doucette built the flying trestle bridge. Guide John Yates later led mountaineers Mumm and Collie along today's North Boundary Trail.

ISBN 978-1-926855-24-0 RMBooks

Each volume contains a complete up-to-date trail guide for the routes discussed, as well as current and historical images and biographies of important figures.

These books are available from Emerson Sanford at emsanf@telus.net for $22.95 each, including shipping to Canadian addresses at no additional charge.

ISBN 978-0-9879270-0-2

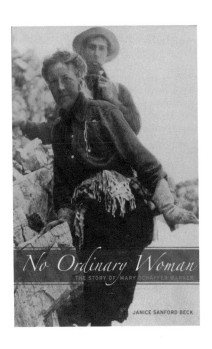

No Ordinary Woman
The Story of Mary Schäffer Warren
by
Janice Sanford Beck

Artist, Photographer, writer, world traveller and, above all, explorer, Mary Schäffer Warren overcame the limited expectations of women at the turn of the 19th century in order to follow her dreams.

ISBN 978-0-921102-82-3

Color and Black and White Photos

$24.95, Softcover

www.rmbooks.com